Bookshelves & Storage Units

BY HERBERT LEAVY

GROSSET
GOOD LIFE
BOOKS

PUBLISHERS · GROSSET & DUNLAP · NEW YORK
A FILMWAYS COMPANY

Cover photograph by Mort Engel.

Acknowledgments

We wish to express our deep appreciation to the following persons and organizations for their very real help in the preparation of this book: Mrs. Maryann Ezell of the American Plywood Association; Ed Benfield of The Stanley Works; Ray Moholt of Western Wood Products Association; David Kellogg of the Southern Forest Products Association; Masonite and Leo Flores of Selz, Seabolt and Associates; Pamela Allsebrook of the California Redwood Association; Donald Meyers, Dick and Arlene Demske for their research facilities. And many thanks to Douglas Corcoran and Larry Gadd of Grosset & Dunlap for their excellent editorial guidance.

To my four daughters—Karen, Kathy, Jill, and Jackie—who have been the inspiration for much shelving and storage building in my home

Contents

Desk and hanging in bookshelves of 1×12-inch western pine divide and conquer space in long narrow bedroom.

Handsome redwood shelves and magazine rack give extra storage space.

Introduction

The "Murphy's Law" of storage is that all available storage space is filled quickly with things that become essential enough to forbid their removal, therefore necessitating more storage space. We can't correct the law, but we can show you how to add more storage space to your home or apartment. The projects within this book have been chosen carefully to allow you the widest range of types of storage—some of them are for rather specialized storage, but almost all can be adapted to your particular needs.

We open with a chapter on how to work with plywood. And most of what you see there can be adapted to any type of wood. It is a good basic instruction section which you will find invaluable prior to attempting any of the projects that follow. Information on wood finishing is also included.

You might want to make some of these projects from prefinished plywood. It will save you the finishing step, which is about half the work. To do this, however, you must be a neat worker so that you don't mar the finish. If you are skilled at woodworking and are careful when you build, this may be the way to go for you, but try it first with small projects.

These storage and shelving projects are fun, and not difficult at all. You can build most of them in a weekend or two. All are portable to some extent, so if you move, you can take most of them with you! Good luck and happy woodworking!

Built-in redwood shelves and storage units in this children's bedroom encourage order and neatness.

6   *Bookshelves & Storage Units*

1
How to Work with Plywood

You can get fir plywood, lumber, and other materials for the projects shown in this book from your local lumberyard. While the materials list given with each project specifies both the type and grade to use, there are a few facts to bear in mind when buying plywood for any building or remodeling job.

Fir plywood comes in two types—exterior and interior. Exterior plywood is made with 100-percent waterproof glue. Use it for outdoor projects, as well as for indoor projects that will be exposed to moisture. Interior plywood is highly moisture resistant but is not made with waterproof glue. Use it for indoor jobs, such as cabinets and furniture.

Both types of plywood have several appearance grades. Use the A-A or its alternate, the A-B grade, when both sides will be in view. Use the Int-DFPA A-D grade when only one side of the panel will be seen.

Laying Out Plywood for Cutting

The big size in which plywood is made simplifies every step of construction. The only step that has to precede actual construction is laying out the work for cutting.

It's worthwhile to do this with care—to avoid waste and simplify your work. When many pieces are to be cut from one panel, you'll find it's easiest to sketch the arrangement on a piece of paper before marking the plywood for cutting. Be sure to allow for a saw kerf (the width of the cut made by the saw) between adjacent pieces.

Try to work it out so that your first cuts reduce the panel to pieces small enough for easy handling.

One of the most important points to watch in planning your sequence of operations is to cut all mating or matching parts with the same saw setting.

Watch the direction of the face grain when cutting. Unless otherwise indicated in the plan, you'll usually want this to run the long way of the piece. Mark on the better face of the plywood unless you are going to cut it with a portable power saw; in that case, mark it on the back.

Sawing Plywood

When using a portable power saw, place the plywood with the good face down. If you tack a strip of scrap lumber to the top of each sawhorse, you can saw right through it without damaging the horse. Keep the saw blade sharp.

When hand sawing, place the plywood with the good face up. Use a saw with 10 to 15 points to the inch. Support the panel firmly so it won't sag. You can reduce splitting out of the underside by putting a piece of scrap lumber under it and sawing it along with the plywood. It also helps to hold the saw at a low angle. Most important of all: use a sharp saw.

Planing plywood edges with a plane or jointer is seldom necessary if you make your cuts with a sharp saw blade. If you do any planing, work from both ends of the edge toward the center to avoid tearing out plies at the end of the cut. Use a plane with a sharp blade; take very shallow cuts.

When power sawing with a radial or table saw, place the plywood with the good face up. Use a sharp combination blade or a fine-toothed one without much set. Let the blade protrude above the plywood just the height of the teeth. You'll find handling large panels by yourself easier if you build an extension support with a roller. It can have a base of its own or may be clamped to a sawhorse.

Sanding before sealer or prime coat is applied should be confined to edges. Fir plywood is sanded smooth during manufacture (this is one of the big timesavers in its use), and further sanding of the surfaces would remove the soft grain. After sealing, sand in the direction of the grain only.

Fir Plywood Construction Joints

Butt joints, like the one in this picture, are the simplest to make and are suitable for ¾" plywood. For thinner panels, use a reinforcing block or nailing strip to make a stronger joint. In both cases, glue makes the joint many times stronger than if it were made with nails or screws alone.

Dado joints, quickly made with a power saw, produce neat shelves. Use a dado blade shimmed out to produce these grooves in a single cut.

Frame construction makes it possible to reduce weight by using thinner plywood since it has amazing strength. Glue as recommended.

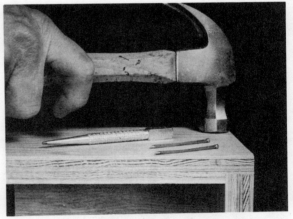

Rabbet joints like this one are strong and easy to make with power tools. You'll find this an ideal joint for drawers, buffets, chests, or cupboards.

Fir Plywood Fasteners

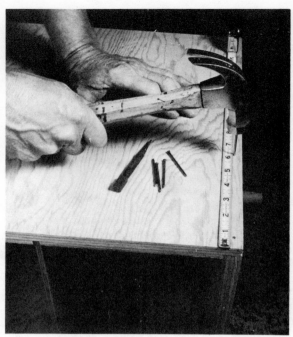

Nail size is determined primarily by the thickness of the plywood you're using. Used with glue, all nails shown here produce strong joints. For ¾" plywood, use 6d casing nails or 6d finishing nails. For ⅝" plywood, use 6d or 8d finishing nails. For ½" plywood, use 4d or 6d finishing nails. For ⅜" plywood, use 3d or 4d finishing nails. For ¼" plywood, use ¾" or 1" brads, 3d finishing nails, or (for backs where there is no objection to heads showing) 1" blue lath nails. Substitute casing for finishing nails wherever you want a heavier nail.

Space nails about 6" apart for most work. Closer spacing is necessary only with thin plywood, where there may be slight buckling between nails. The nails and glue work together to produce a strong, durable joint.

Predrilling is occasionally called for when nails must be placed very close to an edge. As indicated here, the drill bit should have a slightly smaller diameter than the nail to be used.

Flathead wood screws are useful where nails do not provide adequate holding power. Glue should also be used if possible. The sizes shown here are minimums; use longer screws when the work permits. The following list gives the plywood thickness, the diameter and length of the smallest screws recommended, and the length of the hole to drill.

Plywood thickness	Screw diameter	Screw length	Hole length
¾"	No. 8	1½"	⁵⁄₃₂"
⅝"	No. 8	1¼"	⁵⁄₃₂"
½"	No. 6	1¼"	⅛"
⅜"	No. 6	1"	⅛"
¼"	No. 4	¾"	⁷⁄₆₄"

Countersink screws and nails and fill the holes with wood dough or surfacing putty. Apply filler until it is slightly higher than the plywood; sand level when dry. Lubricate screws with soap if they are hard to drive. Avoid damage to plywood surfaces by using Phillips head screws.

Apply glue with a brush or stick. End grain absorbs glue so quickly that it is best to apply a preliminary coat. Allow the preliminary coat to soak in for a few minutes. Then apply another coat before joining the parts.

Gluing

Choose your glue from the chart. Before applying it, make sure of a good fit by testing the joint (below). For lasting strength, both pieces should make contact at all points.

Clamp the joints tightly with clamps (as shown), nails, screws, or other fasteners. Use blocks of wood under the jaws of the clamps to avoid damage to the plywood. Wipe off excess glue, since some glues stain wood and make it difficult to achieve a good finish. Test for squareness and then allow the glue to set.

Assembling

Planning pays off in assembling just as it does in cutting parts. Frequently, the easiest solution is to break down complicated projects into smaller assembly units. They are simpler to handle and make joints more accessible. Apply clamps with the full jaw length in contact. When the jaws are not parallel, as at right in picture, pressure is applied to only part of the joint.

Special clamps frequently save work and help you do a better job. Here are various types of edge clamps used to glue wood or plastic edging to plywood. Bar clamps or quick C-clamps grip the panel, which is protected by scrap wood. Then edge clamping fixtures are inserted to bear against the edge-banding material while the glue sets.

Installing

A handy, little-known trick for clamping miter joints in cabinets in shown here. With paper sandwiched between to permit easy removal, glue triangular blocks to the ends and pull together in alignment with clamps. Remove clamps after the glue has set, pry the blocks away, and sand off the paper.

Hollow masonry walls call for use of toggle bolts or "Molly" fasteners (shown here). Drill the hole with a star drill or carbide-tipped bit. Then insert the Molly and tighten it. After that, you can remove the bolt and use it to hang the cabinet.

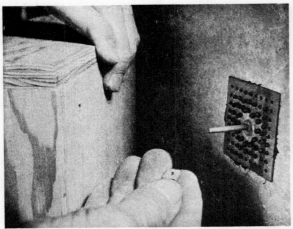

Concrete, stone, or other solid masonry walls call for anchor bolts like this one. Fasten the base to the wall with black mastic, letting it squeeze through the holes. Hang the plywood unit after the mastic has set, using washers. Toggle bolts in expansion shields also may be used.

An additional strip of wood, glued and nailed to the front panel, reinforces the bottom of this second type of drawer made with hand tools. The reinforcing permits the use of economical ¼" fir plywood for the drawer bottoms.

Drawer Construction: Drawers Made with Hand Tools

Drawers Made with Power Tools

This drawer, shown upside down, is made easily with a saw and hammer. Butt joints are glued and nailed. The bottom should be ⅜" or ½" fir plywood for rigidity. The drawer front extends down to cover the front edge of the bottom.

Power tools make it easy to build sturdy drawers. The picture shows one side (dadoed on outer face for drawer guide) being put into place. Rabbet drawer front (at right) to take sides; dado sides to fit drawer back. All four parts are grooved to take ¼" plywood bottom.

Two types of guides, both calling for the use of power tools, are shown in these photographs. As shown at left, the drawer side has been plowed before assembly to fit over a strip that is glued to the side of the cabinet. The procedure is reversed for the version at right, where the cabinet side has been dadoed before assembly. A matching strip is glued to the side of the drawer. Even heavy drawers slide easily on guides like these if they are waxed or lubricated with paraffin after finishing.

Only hand tools are required to make this drawer. The secret is its bottom, made of ⅜" or ½" plywood. The bottom extends ⅜" beyond the sides of the drawer to form a lip. Ease edges and apply paraffin for easy operation.

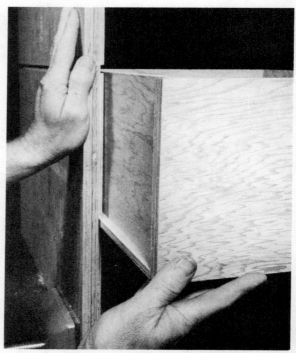

Extended bottom of the drawer described above fits into slots formed by gluing pieces of ⅜" plywood to the inner surface of each side of the cabinet. A gap just wide enough to take the lip is left between the pieces.

Power tools permit making a stronger and lighter version of the same drawer. The bottom is ¼" plywood cut ⅜" wider than the drawer on each side.

This drawer slides in slots dadoed into the ¾" plywood sides of the cabinet. When power tools are used, this is one of the simplest of all methods of drawer-and-guide construction.

Shelf Hanging and Sliding Doors

The neatest and strongest ways to hang a shelf are by making a dado joint or by using metal shelf supports. A dado requires power tools and does not permit changing shelf height. Inexpensive shelf supports plug into blind holes ⅝" deep that are drilled in the plywood sides of the cabinet. Drill additional holes to permit moving the shelves when desired. Another device is the use of slotted metal shelf strips, into which shelf supports may be plugged at any height. For a better fit, set shelf strips flush in a dado cut or cut out shelves around shelf strips.

For removable doors, plow the bottom grooves 3/16" deep and the top grooves ⅜" deep. After finishing, insert the door by pushing up into excess space in top groove and then dropping into bottom. Plowing can be simplified by using a fiber track made for sliding doors of this type. Only hand tools are required when one version of the sliding door is used. Front and back strips are stock ¼" quarter-round molding. The strip between is ¼" square. Use glue and either brads or finish nails to fasten the strips securely.

When hand tools are used, attach strips of ¼″ quarter-round molding for the back to rest against. Glue and nail back to the molding.

Cabinet Backs

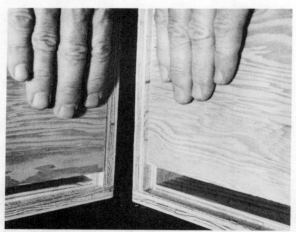

The standard method of applying backs to cabinets and other storage units calls for rabbeting sides. The cabinet at the left in this picture has rabbet just deep enough to take the plywood back. For large units that must fit against walls that may not be perfectly smooth or plumb, the version at the right in this photograph is better. This rabbet is made ½″ or even ¾″ deep. The lip that remains after the back has been inserted may be trimmed easily wherever necessary to get a good fit between the plywood unit and house wall.

Shown here are two methods of applying cabinet backs without rabbets or moldings. One method requires nailing the back flush with the outside edge. The second method requires setting the back ½″ to ⅞″ away from the edges. The back becomes inconspicuous when the cabinet is against the wall.

Bevel cabinet backs that must applied without a rabbet to make them less conspicuous. Install a ⅜″ plywood back flush with the edges of the cabinet and then bevel with light strokes of a block plane.

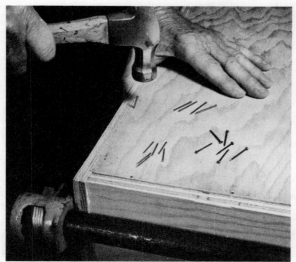

Nail the cabinet back into rabbet by driving nails at a slight angle, as indicated here. Use 1" brads or 4d finish nails. Where back will not be seen, the 1" blue lath nails shown here may be used.

Edge Treatment

You can achieve handsome, solid, finished plywood edges by cutting a V groove and inserting a matching wood strip, but this method is comparatively difficult.

Two-hand staplers like this one are excellent for nailing cabinet backs. They drive long staples, setting them below the surface if desired, and greatly speed up the work. They are sometimes available on loan or rental.

Thin strips of real-wood edge banding are available already coated with pressure-sensitive adhesive. Peel off the backing paper and apply to plywood edges according to the manufacturer's recommendations. The photograph shows one edge already covered with a strip of Douglas fir to match plywood.

Laminated plastic surfacing materials may be applied to edges of tables with the same contact cement applied to tabletops. As shown at lower right, apply to edges first, then to the countertop or tabletop. A thicker, more massive effect can be achieved by nailing a 1" or 1¼" strip all around the underneath edge.

To fill the end grain on plywood edges that are to be painted, several varieties of wood putty are available either powdered (to be mixed with water) or prepared (ready for use). Plaster spackling also works well. Sand smooth when thoroughly dry and then finish.

Pulls, Handles, and Catches

Drawer pulls and door handles of the types shown here are widely available. Use them in metal or wood to style your project. They come in a variety of traditional and ranch styles, as well as in many modern designs.

The simplest drawer pull of all is a notch cut into the top of the drawer front. It may be rectangular, V-shaped, or half-round. You can omit the notch from every other drawer, opening it by means of the notch in the drawer below, as shown. If you slope the drawer fronts, the drawer may be pulled out by grasping the projecting bottom edge.

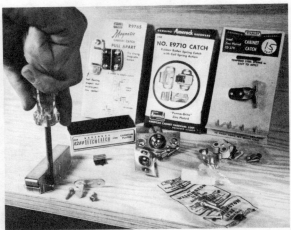

Sliding and rolling doors are equipped most easily with finger cups that you simply force into round holes. For large doors, use rectangular cups or large round ones that are fastened in with screws. Round pulls at top are suitable where clearance is adequate, or you can make simple rectangular grips from wood.

Catches come in many varieties besides the conventional friction type shown at the extreme right in this picture. The touch type, being installed here, lets the door open at a touch. Magnetic catches have no moving parts to break. Roller catches and the new ones made of polyethylene are smoother and more durable than plain steel friction catches.

Door Hardware

Surface hinges are mounted quickly. They require no mortising, add an ornamental touch, and come in many styles. A pair of H or H-L hinges will do for most doors; for large doors or to add rigidity to small ones, use a pair of H-L plus one H (as shown here) or use three of the H type. Tee or strap hinges help prevent sag in large doors. On tall doors, one or two hinges added between those at the top and bottom help to minimize warping.

Concealed pin hinges give a neat modern appearance to flush doors. They mount directly onto the cabinet side. Construction is simplified, because no face frame is necessary. Only the pivot is visible from the front when the door is closed. Use a pair for small doors and 3 (called "a pair and one-half") for large doors.

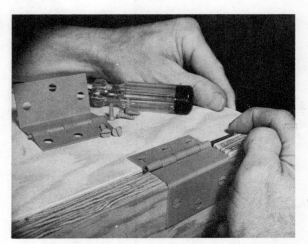

Overlapping (lipped) doors are neatly hung with semiconcealed hinges. They are excellent for plywood, since screws go into flat grain. These have a ½" inset and are made for doors of ¾" plywood rabbeted to leave a ¼" lip. Such hinges are made in many styles and finishes, semiconcealed or full surface.

Semiconcealed loose-pin hinges like these appear the same when the door is closed as ordinary butt hinges, since only the barrel shows. They're much better, though, for flush plywood doors, because screws go into flat plywood grain. A variation called a chest hinge may be used in the same way.

Two metal brackets fasten to the top of each door with a pair of screws. Nylon wheels with ball bearings roll in a double-lipped track that is fastened to the door frame with screws. (A single-lipped track is made for single doors.) Installation is simple, with no mortising required.

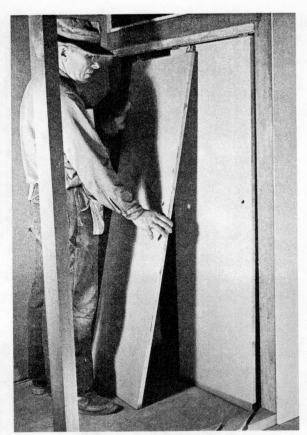

Rolling doors for closets and large storage units may have rollers mounted at either the top or bottom. Top-mount hardware, shown in these three pictures, is usually smoother in operation, particularly when the door is tall and narrow.

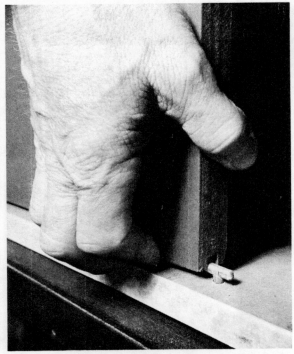

Door bottoms are kept in line by a simple T-guide for each door. Two strips of ¼" quarter-round molding, with ¼" space between, can be used to form a slot if power tools are not available for making it.

How to Fasten Anything to Any Wall

Most walls are made of a framework of 2 × 4's, called studs, covered with either wood or metal lath and either plaster or wallboard, as shown above. The studs are placed 16 inches apart from center to center in most cases. You can't see them, of course, since they're covered with plaster or wallboard. But if you can find one, it's likely that there's another one 16 inches away. The reason you want to find them is to screw whatever you're fastening to the wall right to a good, solid piece of wood.

One far from foolproof way to find a stud is to lightly tap the wall with a hammer until you hear a "solid" sound. Another telltale sign of studs is to look along the baseboard to see where it's nailed. Usually there will be a stud at that point, especially if the next nail is 16 inches away. When you find a likely looking nail, use your level to project the position up the wall to the right location.

If all this sounds like a lot of trouble, you can compromise by using one of the many kinds of wall fasteners (Molly bolts) that expand behind the plaster or wallboard. These fasteners are okay for almost anything you want to hang, except for very weighty pieces. One thing, though: before you drill the big hole for the fastener, drill a little hole for a screw, just in case you hit a stud!

If you need to fasten something to a masonry wall, like the concrete block walls in your basement, there are a number of methods. You can drill a hole with a carbide-tipped masonry bit in your electric drill and then insert lead or fiber plugs. Then drive screws into the plugs, expanding them inside the holes for a friction fit. Special hardened steel nails also work fairly well in concrete block.

The newest and one of the best ways to fasten to masonry is to use builder's adhesive. This works best on dry, unpainted masonry, but it holds very well on most painted surfaces, too. This adhesive comes in a tube and is applied with a caulking gun. Just put a bead of adhesive along the strip to be glued to the wall, stick the strip in place, and then pull the strip away again to put a layer of adhesive on the wall. Let both pieces dry for 10 minutes before putting the strip back to stay.

2
Sidestep Storage

Here's a fun way to combine book learning with colorful play furniture. And youngsters will find more than enough space for their books, games, dolls, model airplanes, and ant farms. Highly attractive, versatile, and practical, this storage unit is also easy to build.

Instructions

1. Cut plywood panels to the exact sizes shown in the cutting diagram. This operation can be done best with a table saw. If none is available, use a skill saw. (Be sure to use a straight edge as a guide for your skill saw.) Although a table or skill saw will do the job best, a good hand saw or saber saw will do.

2. Sand all edges, using #50 grit sandpaper. If rounded edges on the step rails are desired, do them now. A sanding block will handle this operation.

3. At this point, assemble all the uprights and shelves. Make any find adjustments now to get a good fit.

4. When ready to fasten the assembly, use a good woodworking glue and finishing nails. Toenail the finishing nails at the front and back of the unit. Countersink the nail heads.

5. Cut the ¼" plywood backs and attach as shown in the illustration. This adds the necessary stability to the unit. Use 1" box nails and glue to fasten these pieces.

6. Fill all visible voids and countersunk nail heads with spackle. Allow spackle to dry and then sand with #120 grit sandpaper.

7. Fill all exposed plywood edges with natural paste wood filler. This will seal all the edge voids and give a smooth surface when painted.

8. The storage unit is now ready for painting. Several colors may be used. Paint the door and desk top separately. A latex paint is easily applied, although an enamel paint is usually more durable. A nice touch is to cover the desk top with formica.

9. Mount the door and desk top with hinges, magnetic catches, eye hooks, and chains.

Materials List

Plywood
4 panels, ¾″ × 4′ × 8′, A-A or A-B INT-DFPA
1 panel, ¼″ × 4′ × 8′, A-D INT-DFPA

Other Materials
2″   finishing nails
1½″ finishing nails
1″   box nails
Spackle
Natural paste wood filler
Woodworking glue
#50 grit and #120 grit sandpaper
Paint (colors as desired)
2 pairs of hinges, 1½″ × 2″ (cabinet butt)
3′ decorative small-link chain
4 medium-sized eye hooks
3 magnetic catches
2 decorative knobs

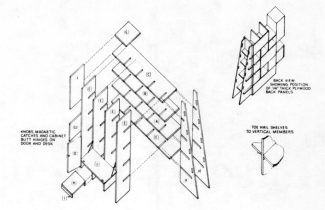

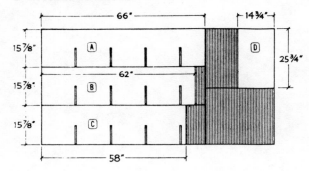

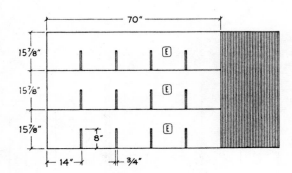

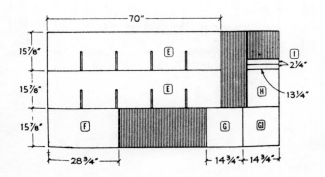

CUTTING DIAGRAM

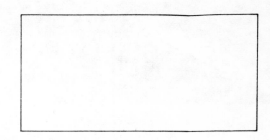

¼″ x 48″x 96″ PLYWOOD FOR BACK
COVER PANELS (CUT TO FIT)

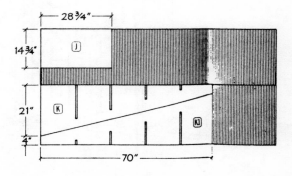

ALL PANELS ¾″x 48″x 96″ PLYWOOD
UNLESS OTHERWISE NOTED.

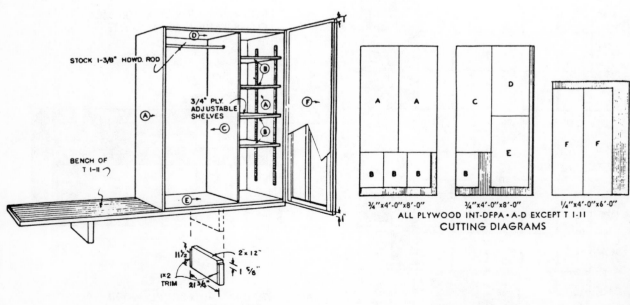

STOCK 1-3/8" HDWD. ROD

3/4" PLY.
ADJUSTABLE
SHELVES

BENCH OF
T 1-11

11½"

1×2
TRIM

21¾"

2"×12"

1 5/8"

A

A

C

D

E

B

B

B

B

F

F

¾"×4'-0"×8'-0"

¾"×4'-0"×8'-0"

¼"×4'-0"×6'-0"

ALL PLYWOOD INT-DFPA • A-D EXCEPT T 1-11
CUTTING DIAGRAMS

3
Entry Closet

This practical full-length entry closet set on a bench also makes an attractive room divider. Build it with versatile plywood in just a few hours.

Instructions

1. Cut plywood pieces to size.
2. Nail and glue sides A to top D and bottom E. Install divider C. Use white glue that comes in plastic squeeze bottle.
3. Trim lap from Texture 1–11 panels. Fit and nail Texture 1–11 back panel in place.
4. To assemble the doors, nail 1″ × 2″ stiffeners around edges of each door and down center. Keep stiffener 2″ from hinged side edge and 1″ from other edges.
5. Nail ¼″ backs F to 1″ × 2″ stiffeners.
6. Nail 2″ × 2″ framing and mitered 1″ × 2″ edging around bench top. Attach to legs.
7. Finish to suit. Install hardware and assemble.

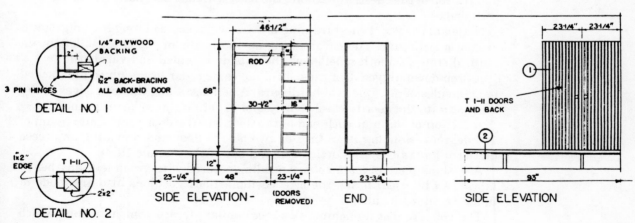

DETAIL NO. I

DETAIL NO. 2

SIDE ELEVATION - (DOORS REMOVED)

END

SIDE ELEVATION

PARTS SCHEDULE

CODE	NO. REQ'D	SIZE	PART IDENTIFICATION
A	2	23¾″x68″	End
B	4	14″x22″	Shelf
C	1	22″x66½″	Divider
D	1	23¾″x45″	Top
E	1	23¾″x45″	Bottom
F	2	21¼″x66″	Door Backing
	2 Pcs.	24″ x 68″	T 1-11 Doors
	1 pc.	48″ x 68″	T 1-11 Back
	1 pc.	24″ x 91½″	T 1-11 Bench

50 Lin. Ft. 1″x2″ Door Stiffeners and Bench Edging; 28 Lin. Ft. 2″x2″ Bench Framing; 2¾ Lin. Ft. 1⅜″ Diameter Hardwood Rod; 4 Lin. Ft. 2″x12″ Bench Legs; 20 Lin. Ft. Adj. Metal Standard; 6 Pin Hinges; 2 Door Pulls; 4 Door Catches.

4
Sofa Bed with Built-in Storage Chest

It is not often that you can build or buy something that serves many purposes, yet is attractive and economical. Such an article of furniture is a combination sofa–guest bed–storage chest that can be built for about $98 in material.

This three-way unit provides comfortable seating atop a spacious cedar-lined storage chest, and with the back cushion removed, it converts into an extra guest bed.

Construction is relatively simple. On a frame of 2 × 4's, attach a standard 3' × 6'8" hollow-core door. Place the door, which forms the bottom of the bed and the top of the chest, flush along the back with a 6" overhang in front and at both ends.

Nailed to the 2 × 4 chest framing are 3½" wide pieces of tongue-and-grooved aromatic red cedar. The cedar lining on the inside of the chest is left in its natural state for moth-repellency; the outside is sealed and varnished.

A drop-down hinged door consists of the same cedar lining glued and tacked to both sides of a ¼" piece of hardboard. A setback along the four edges of the door permits the door to close tightly and to retain the cedar fragrance.

A section of chain at each end of the door lets the door open a maximum of 180 degrees, stopping it an inch or two off the floor and providing an access platform for transferring articles in and out of the storage chest.

A 4"-thick piece of foam-rubber padding covered with green felt (any heavy fabric can be used) forms the seat cushion. Back cushions also are made of upholstered foam rubber.

The bolsters rest up against two rectangular storage compartments, which are built on a light wood frame covered with ¼" hardboard and upholstered to match the bolsters and seat cushion. The compartments act as spacers to narrow the width of the bed when it's used as a sofa, and with openings in the back to provide storage for pillows and bedding.

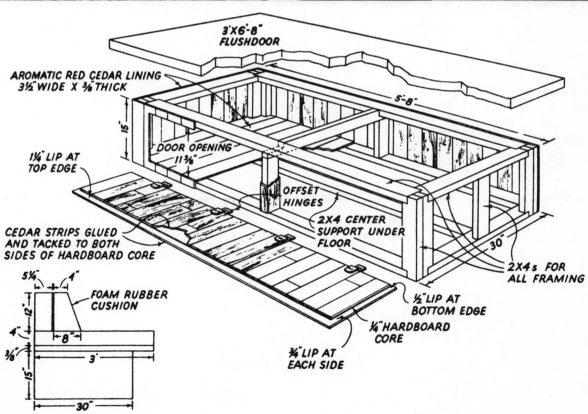

3'X6'-8" FLUSHDOOR

AROMATIC RED CEDAR LINING 3½" WIDE X ⅜" THICK

5'-8"

15"

1¼" LIP AT TOP EDGE

DOOR OPENING 11⅜"

OFFSET HINGES

2X4 CENTER SUPPORT UNDER FLOOR

CEDAR STRIPS GLUED AND TACKED TO BOTH SIDES OF HARDBOARD CORE

30"

2X4s FOR ALL FRAMING

½" LIP AT BOTTOM EDGE

¼" HARDBOARD CORE

¾" LIP AT EACH SIDE

5¼" 4"

FOAM RUBBER CUSHION

12"

4"

8"

⅜"

3'

15"

30"

Type of glue	Description	Recommended use	Precautions	How to use
Hide glue	Comes as flakes to be heated in water or in prepared form as liquid hide glue. Light color. Very strong and tough.	Excellent for furniture and cabinet work. Gives strength even to joints that do not fit very well.	Not waterproof; do not use for outdoor furniture or anything exposed to weather or dampness.	Apply in a warm room to both surfaces and let it become tacky before joining. Clamp for 3 hours.
Urea resin glue	Comes as powder to be mixed with water and used within 4 hours. Light color. Very strong if joint fits well.	Good for general wood gluing. First choice for work that must stand some exposure to dampness, since it is almost waterproof.	Needs well-fitted joints, tight clamping, and room temperature 70° or warmer.	Make sure joints fit tightly. Mix glue and apply a thin coat. Allow 16 hours drying time.
Liquid resin (white) glue	Comes ready to use at any temperature. Clean-working, quick setting. Strong enough for most work though not quite as tough as hide glue.	Good for indoor furniture and cabinetwork. First choice for small jobs where clamping or good fit may be difficult.	Not sufficiently resistant to moisture for outdoor furniture or for outdoor storage units.	Use at any temperature but preferably one above 60°. Spread on both surfaces and clamp at once. Sets in 1½ hours.
Resorcinol (waterproof) glue	Comes as powder plus liquid to be mixed each time used. Dark color. Very strong and completely waterproof.	This is the glue to use with exterior-type plywood for work to be exposed to extreme dampness.	Expense, trouble to mix, and dark color make it unsuited to jobs where waterproof glue is not required.	Use within 8 hours after mixing. Work at temperature above 70°. Apply a thin coat to both surfaces. Allow 16 hours drying time.

5
Under-eave Storage

Here's an easy-to-build plywood built-in used to transform that awkward space under a sloping ceiling into one of the most useful areas in your home. It's designed for remodeling expansion attics or for use in story-and-a-half homes with sloping upstairs ceilings. By cutting the sides to the proper angle, it can be made to fit any ceiling slope.

Even amateurs will find no difficulty in building this under-eave storage. Easy-to-follow plans and directions show construction steps clearly from start to finish.

Instructions

1. Lay out all plywood parts and cut to size, allowing for saw kerfs. Make sure that the top edge of sides and partitions are cut to the proper angle to fit slope of ceiling and that center partition is notched as shown for beveled 1 × 2 frame.

2. Using 6d finishing nails and glue, apply 3″ plywood base strips to bottom. Before installing sides and partitions, cut shelf cleats to length and fasten in positions shown with countersunk screws. Tilt up bottom so that the front edge rests on floor and fasten left side, back, and partition between wardrobe and drawer space. Apply glue and then, with ½″ plywood partition in position, nail through bottom and adjacent partition. The partition to the right of the drawer space is installed similarly. Be sure to keep entire assembly in perfect square as you glue the 1 × 2 frame along the top and nail it into place.

3. If the floor is uneven, level the assembly after sliding it into position. Nail into place with 8d finishing nails through ½″ plywood back into studs.

4. Install plywood support for clothes pole in wardrobe as shown in detail A or use standard wood escutcheons if desired. Position and fasten plywood shelf above and then shoe racks near floor as shown.

5. Cut drawer guides to length and then apply to shelves with countersunk screws. Fasten back shelves in position behind ½″ plywood partitions.

6. Cut vertical face frames from 1″ stock, apply with 6d nails, and glue. Follow with installation of 12″ face panel on front and triangular-shaped

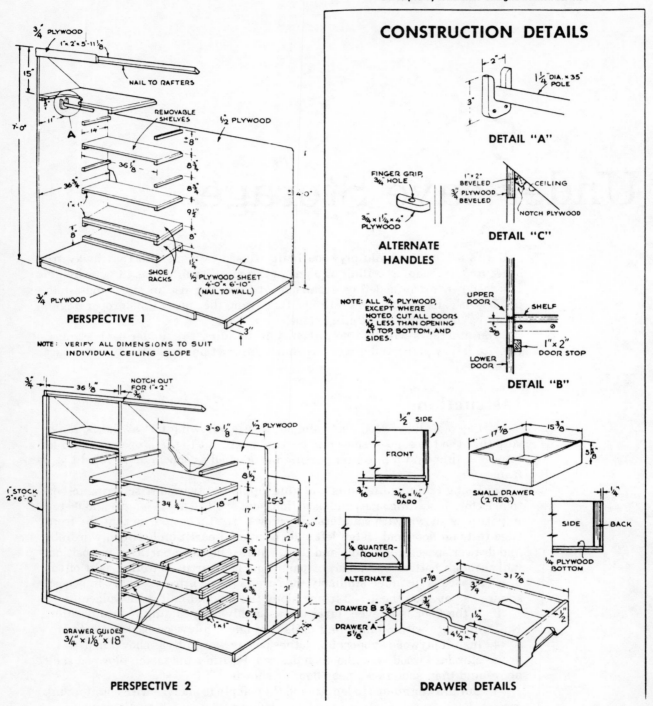

UNDER-EAVE STORAGE

Developed by Iowa State College Extension Service

CONSTRUCTION DETAILS

DETAIL "A"

2"
1¼" DIA. × 35" POLE
3"

ALTERNATE HANDLES

FINGER GRIP, ¾" HOLE
¾" × 1¼" × 4" PLYWOOD

DETAIL "C"

1" × 2" BEVELED
¾" PLYWOOD BEVELED
CEILING
NOTCH PLYWOOD

NOTE: ALL ¾" PLYWOOD, EXCEPT WHERE NOTED. CUT ALL DOORS ¹⁄₁₆ LESS THAN OPENING AT TOP, BOTTOM, AND SIDES.

DETAIL "B"

UPPER DOOR
SHELF
⅜"
LOWER DOOR
1" × 2" DOOR STOP

½" SIDE
FRONT
³⁄₁₆" ¼"
DADO
³⁄₁₆

17⅞" 15⅜"
5⅝"
SMALL DRAWER (2 REQ.)

¼" QUARTER-ROUND
ALTERNATE

¼"
SIDE BACK
¼" PLYWOOD BOTTOM

17⅞" 31⅞"
¾"
¾"
DRAWER B 5¾"
DRAWER A 5⅛"
1½"
4½"
½"

DRAWER DETAILS

PERSPECTIVE 1

¾" PLYWOOD
1" × 2" × 5-11⅛"
NAIL TO RAFTERS
15"
7'-0"
11"
A
14"
REMOVABLE SHELVES
½" PLYWOOD
±8"
36⅛"
8¾"
36¾"
8¾"
9½"
1" × 4"
8"
8"
SHOE RACKS
1¼"
½" PLYWOOD SHEET 4'-0" × 6'-10" (NAIL TO WALL)
4'-0"
¾" PLYWOOD
3"

NOTE: VERIFY ALL DIMENSIONS TO SUIT INDIVIDUAL CEILING SLOPE

PERSPECTIVE 2

¾"
36⅛"
NOTCH OUT FOR 1" × 2" ¾"
½" PLYWOOD
3'-9⅛"
1" STOCK 2" × 6'-9"
8½"
34¼" 18"
17"
5'-3"
4'-0"
6¾"
12"
6"
6¾"
21"
6¾"
1" × 1"
DRAWER GUIDES ¾" × 1⅛" × 18"
17⅛"

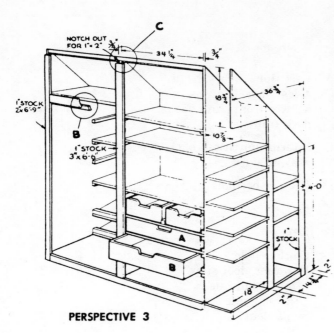

PERSPECTIVE 3

panels over shelves and door on right side.

7. Dado and rabbet drawer parts and then assemble and fit as shown in drawer details.

8. Cut and apply horizontal face frames from ¾″ plywood. Be sure to install 1 × 2 door stops where required.

9. Hang doors using semiconcealed cabinet hinges. Install friction catches, metal chains for drop shelf, and door pulls.

10. Ease and sand all edges with 1–0 paper. Remove door pulls, fill nailing holes with spackle or wood paste, and prepare for finishing by sanding with 3–0 paper.

11. Paint or finish as desired, but follow the recommendations given closely. Be very careful to finish door edges thoroughly and to apply equal coats to front and back faces. After finishing, install adjustable shelf standards and replace door pulls.

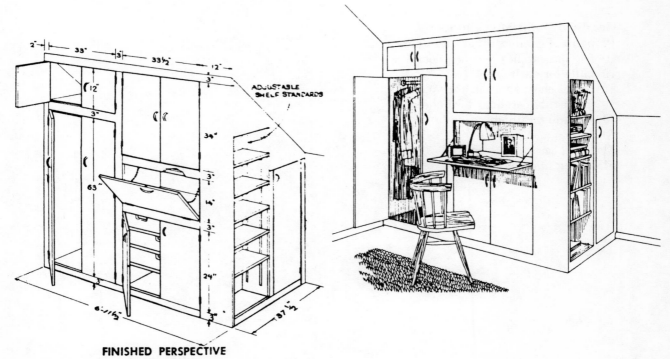

FINISHED PERSPECTIVE

Materials List

Plywood

No.	Size	Type	Where used
7 panels	4′ × 8′ × ¾″	Interior DFPA A–A	Partitions, doors, front, sides, floor, shelves, drawer fronts and backs, desk front
2 panels	4′ × 8′ × ½″	Interior DFPA A–D	Interior partition, back, drawer sides
1 piece	4′ × 4′ × ¼″	Interior DFPA A–D	Drawer bottoms

Lumber

Length	Size	Use
3′	1¼″ diameter	Clothes pole
12′	1 × 2	Framing, door stop, miscellaneous
12′	¾ × 1⅛	Drawer guides
44′	1 × 1	Shelf cleats

Hardware and Miscellaneous
12 pairs of cabinet hinges for doors
10 friction catches for each door
10 pulls for each door
 2 metal chains for each drop shelf
18′ adjustable standard for shelves
4d, 6d, and 8d finishing nails
Glue
Flathead screws as required
Finishing materials

6
Freestanding Storage Wall

This freestanding unit may be placed against any interior wall or partition, and it provides something nice to look at and a lot of storage space. It has special sections for sound equipment, magazines, and books; a fold-down desk with cubbyholes and drawers; a bar unit; and closed, sliding-door units. Verticals are Texture 1–11 (grooved) plywood, so you can slide the shelves and units in at varying heights and adjust them as desired.

Instructions

Vary the cutting diagrams and parts schedule for the number of bays, units, and shelves required. As a room divider, each bay may be used from either side, since plywood backs are interchangeable. Install hi-fidelity components in plywood units for conversion to a music wall and use the magazine unit for record storage.

1. Allow for saw kerfs as you lay out all plywood parts to size. Glue and nail cut sections of Texture 1–11 plywood and end panels B to 2×2 standards, leaving a ½″ along edges. Do not fasten bottom pieces of Texture 1–11 or cross members until tops O and bottoms P have been cut, glued, and nailed to hold the first and last two bays together. In this way, each two-bay section can later be moved out of the shop for final assembly in place.

2. Cut backs, shelves, and all component parts of each unit to size and sand mating edges. Tops and bottoms of bar and desk units must have edges rabbeted to depth of 11/16″ so that projecting edge may slide in the grooves. Depth of the rabbet on door edges must be 1⅛″ to clear edges of Texture 1–11 and sides E. Glue and nail ⅜″ × ¾″ facing on bottom edges and then assemble each unit with shelves, drawer guides, and partitions in place. Drill ¾″ finger pulls and assemble drawers for desk unit after fronts have been dadoed and rabbeted. Then install cabinet hardware.

3. Make dado cuts for dividers of magazine unit as shown. Rabbet edges and assemble with nails and glue.

4. The fronts of the drawer units must be rabbeted at sides to a depth of 1⅛″. Make a ⅜″ rabbet at bottom and assemble drawer as shown. Increase depth of

CUTTING DIAGRAMS

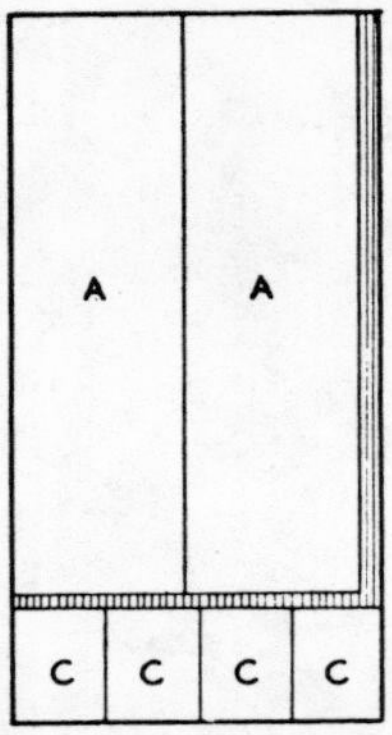

⅜'' x 4'-0'' x 8'-0'' (2 REQ'D)
INTERIOR • DFPA • A-A

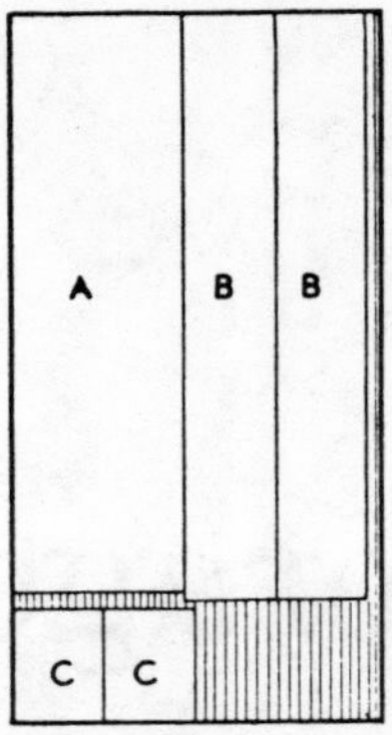

⅜'' x 4'-0'' x 8'-0''
INTERIOR • DFPA • A-A

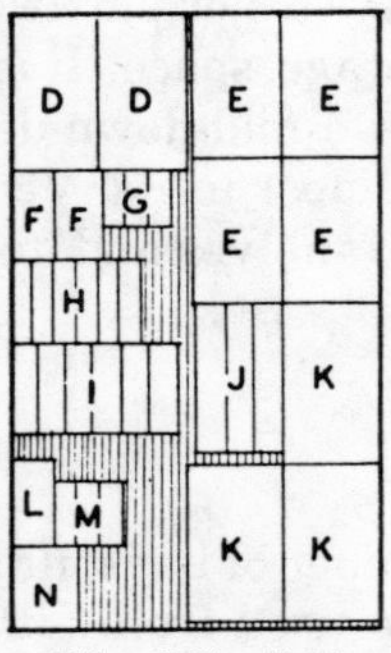

⅜'' x 4'-0'' x 7'-0''
INTERIOR • DFPA • A-D

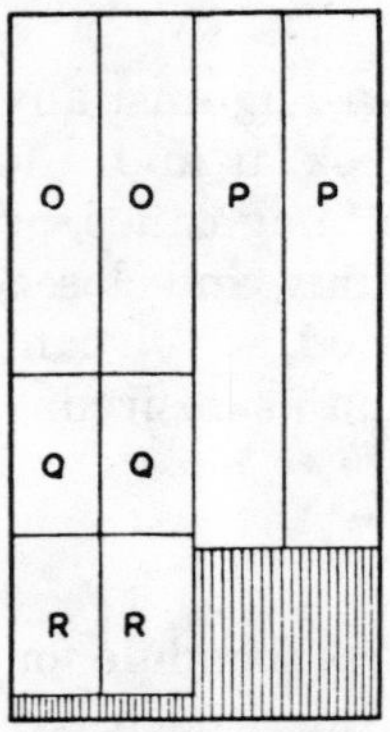

⅝'' x 4'-0'' x 8'-0''
INTERIOR • DFPA • A-D

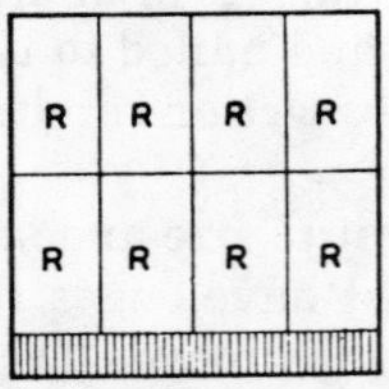

⅝'' x 4'-0'' x 4'-0''
INTERIOR • DFPA • A-D

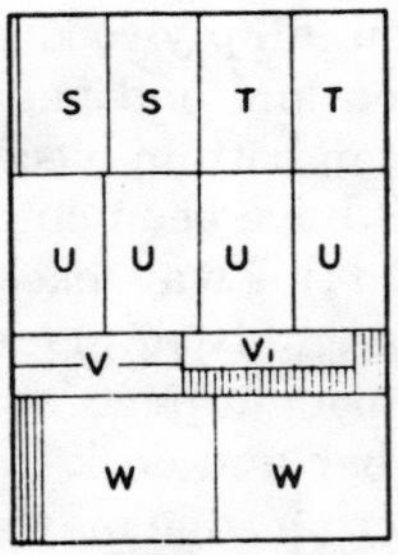

¾'' x 4'-0'' x 6'-0''
INTERIOR • DFPA • A-D

PARTS SCHEDULE

CODE	NO. REQ'D	SIZE	PART IDENTIFICATION
A	5	22⅜'' x 78½''	Back Panel
B	2	11⅞'' x 80⅛''	Side Panel
C	10	11⅞'' x 15⅝''	Magazine Unit Partitions
D	2	11½'' x 21¼''	Bar & Desk Shelf
E	4	11⅞'' x 19⅝''	Bar & Desk Side
F	2	6'' x 11½''	Desk Partition
G	3	2¾'' x 7⅜''	Desk Drawer Back
H	6	2¾'' x 11¼''	Desk Drawer Side
I	6	3⅝'' x 11⅞''	Drawer Unit Side
J	3	3⅝'' x 20¼''	Drawer Unit Back
K	3	11⅞'' x 21⅝''	Drawer Unit Bottom
L	1	3½'' x 11½''	Desk Shelf
M	3	3'' x 9''	Desk Drawer Front
N	1	9'' x 11½''	Desk Partition
O	2	11⅞'' x 48 13/16''	Top & Bottom Shelf
P	2	11⅞'' x 72 13/16''	Top & Bottom Shelf
Q	2	11⅞'' x 21⅝''	Top & Bottom Mag. Unit
R	10	11⅞'' x 21⅝''	Adjustable Shelf
S	2	11½'' x 21⅝''	Top—Bar & Desk
T	2	11⅞'' x 21⅝''	Bottom—Bar & Desk
U	4	11⅞'' x 21⅝''	Top & Bottom—Storage Unit
V	2	4'' x 22⅜''	Front—Drawer Unit
VI	1	4⅜'' x 22⅜''	Front—Top Drawer Unit
W	2	19⅝'' x 22⅜''	Doors—Bar & Desk Unit
X	4	10⅞'' x 11 3/16''	Sliding Doors
Y	3	9'' x 11¼''	Desk Drawer Bottom
	7 Panels	T - 1-11 16/2 - 8'-0''	Grooved Side Panels
	96 Lin. Ft.	2'' x 2'' - 8'-0''	Standards
	8 Lin. Ft.	⅜'' x ½''	Drawer Guides
	12 Lin. Ft.	⅜'' x ¾''	Edge Facing
	4 Lin. Ft.	⅜'' x 1''	Fiber Track
	2 Ea.	—	Magnetic Catches
	2 Pr.	—	Cabinet Hinges
	4 Ea.	10'' Long	Metal Lid Support

Miscellaneous—1'' & 1¼'' No. 6 R.H. screws
4d finish nails and glue
finishing materials as required

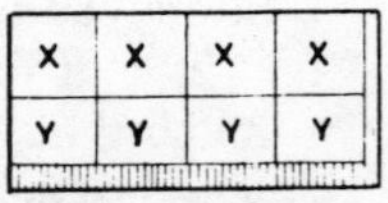

¼'' x 2'-0'' x 4'-0''
DFPA • A-D

top drawer to 4⅜ and rabbet upper edge to fit flush against shelf edge. Drill 1¼″ finger pulls.

5. Rabbet top and bottom edges of storage units. Glue and nail ⅜″ × ¾″ facings to front edges and then make dado cuts for sliding doors and fiber track as shown in sliding door detail. Install doors after drilling 1¼″ finger pulls.

6. Glue and fasten each two-bay section together with 1¼″ No. 6 screws and install backs as shown. Fill any nail holes with wood paste and sand all parts with 3–0 sandpaper.

7. Finish as recommended in harmonizing, contemporary colors.

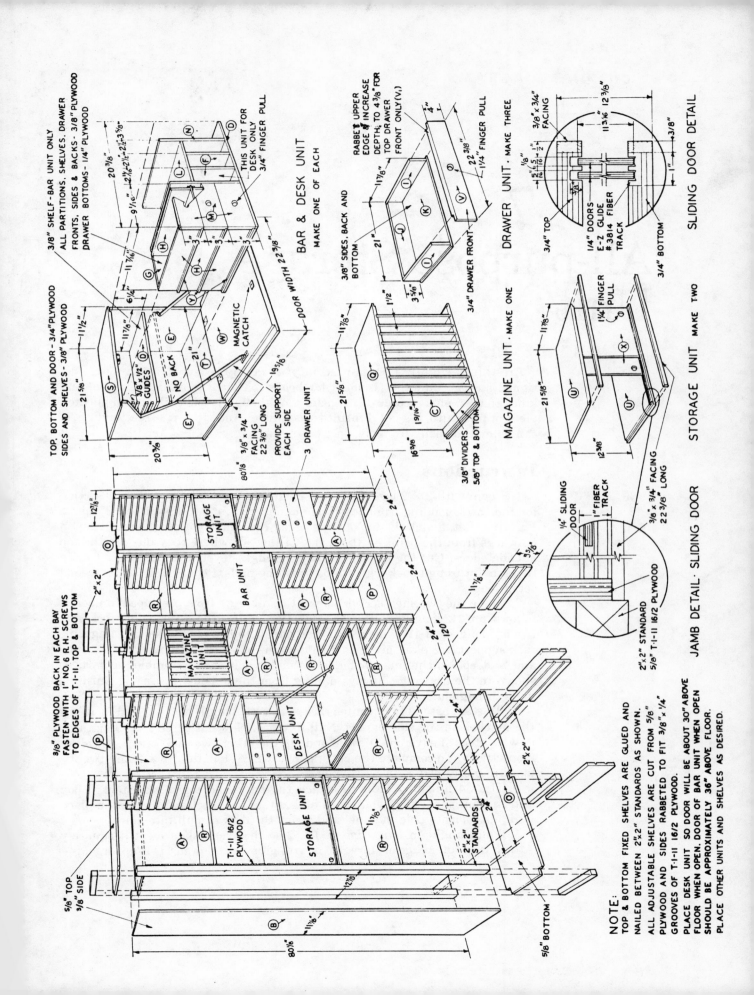

THIS UNIT FOR DESK ONLY

3/8" SHELF-BAR UNIT ONLY
ALL PARTITIONS, SHELVES, DRAWER FRONTS, SIDES & BACKS - 3/8" PLYWOOD
DRAWER BOTTOMS - 1/4" PLYWOOD

TOP, BOTTOM AND DOOR - 3/4" PLYWOOD
SIDES AND SHELVES - 3/8" PLYWOOD

BAR & DESK UNIT
MAKE ONE OF EACH

3/4" FINGER PULL

MAGNETIC CATCH

NO BACK

3/8 x 1/2" GUIDES

DOOR WIDTH 22 3/8"

3/8" x 3/4" FACING 22 3/8" LONG
PROVIDE SUPPORT EACH SIDE

3 DRAWER UNIT

RABBET UPPER EDGE & INCREASE DEPTH TO 4 3/8 FOR TOP DRAWER FRONT ONLY (v.)

3/8" SIDES, BACK AND BOTTOM

1/4" FINGER PULL

3/4" DRAWER FRONT

DRAWER UNIT · MAKE THREE

MAGAZINE UNIT · MAKE ONE

3/8" DIVIDERS
5/8" TOP & BOTTOM

SLIDING DOOR DETAIL

3/8" x 3/4" FACING

1/4" DOORS E-Z GLIDE #3814 FIBER TRACK

3/4" TOP

3/4" BOTTOM

1/4" FINGER PULL

STORAGE UNIT MAKE TWO

JAMB DETAIL · SLIDING DOOR

1/4" SLIDING DOOR

1" FIBER TRACK

3/8" x 3/4" FACING 22 3/8" LONG

2" x 2" STANDARD
5/8" T-I-II 16/2 PLYWOOD

3/8" PLYWOOD BACK IN EACH BAY FASTEN WITH 1" NO. 6 R.H. SCREWS TO EDGES OF T-I-II, TOP & BOTTOM

2" x 2"

80 1/8"

STORAGE UNIT

BAR UNIT

MAGAZINE UNIT

DESK UNIT

STORAGE UNIT

T-I-II 16/2 PLYWOOD

2" x 2" STANDARDS

5/8" TOP
3/8" SIDE

5/8" BOTTOM

80 1/8"

NOTE:
TOP & BOTTOM FIXED SHELVES ARE GLUED AND NAILED BETWEEN 2"x2" STANDARDS AS SHOWN.

ALL ADJUSTABLE SHELVES ARE CUT FROM 5/8" PLYWOOD AND SIDES RABBETED TO FIT 3/8" x 1/4" GROOVES OF T-I-II 16/2 PLYWOOD.

PLACE DESK UNIT SO DOOR WILL BE ABOUT 30" ABOVE FLOOR WHEN OPEN. DOOR OF BAR UNIT WHEN OPEN SHOULD BE APPROXIMATELY 36" ABOVE FLOOR. PLACE OTHER UNITS AND SHELVES AS DESIRED.

7
All-purpose Storage Unit

Are things slightly unorganized in your family room? Here's a newly designed storage unit that is ideal for books, baseball gloves, glassware, and knickknacks, plus records or magazines. Although it looks like a complicated piece of furniture, it's not difficult to assemble. And since it's freestanding, it can be moved easily from one spot to another.

Instructions

1. Begin with 2 × 2 legs. Cut a 61″ length for one back leg and a 64″ section for the corresponding front leg. The outside bottom edges will be 12″ apart. Figuring that, match the top outside edges, and make your long angled cut on both legs from the point on the inside of the "V" where they meet to the top outside edges. Cut the bottom of the 64″ length level with the floor. To join them, nail through back leg with 6d finishing nails. Repeat this for the second set of legs.

2. Make the two shelf sections next. Cut all parts from preripped lumber as follows: ten 12″ lengths of 9″-wide stock; two 56″ lengths of 9¾″-wide stock, and two 56″ lengths of 12″-wide stock. Side panels to be notched for the magazine rack support (see plan) are each 55¼″ lengths of board. Each notch is 1⅝″ long and ¾″ deep. Notches may be made with a keyhole saw. Assemble the parts as shown in the drawings, always nailing from the outside in. Use 54 finishing nails throughout.

3. To start assembly of center rack, cut a 31″ length of 1 × 2 and fit it into the notches on the side panels. Nail in place. Now cut three 29½″ lengths of 9″-wide stock. Leave one 9″ wide and rip the other two to 6″ and 5¼″ widths, respectively. To complete the cutting, cut a 29½″ length of 1 × 2 and twenty-four 18″ pieces of 1 × 1.

4. Use 54 finishing nails to attach the back and top of the storage box. Attach front panel (5¼″ wide) with hinges that are inset and screwed in place. Drill appropriate hole in panel and screw the drawer pull into place.

5. Place angle on long edge of 1 × 2 so that rack slats meet it squarely. Attach it to outer edge of storage box with glue and 2d brads. Cut upper ends of

1×2 slats to fit crosspiece and nail in place with 2d brads, leaving ½" between each slat.

6. Your last assembly job is to attach legs to the unit. This must be done carefully with glue and screws. Begin by drilling three ⅛" holes in each of the legs. Space them evenly along portion flush to side panels. Clean all surfaces to be glued. Apply glue and screw in place, making sure that back leg is flush with back panel and that bottom of first shelf is 24" from floor. Use 2½" No. 8 wood screws.

7. When glue dries, clean away excess. Sand entire unit lightly. Set and fill nail holes. Paint or stain, as desired.

Materials List

2 12' pieces of 2×2
2 12' pieces of 1×10 (ripped at yard to 9" width)
2 10' pieces of 1×11 (ripped at yard to 9¾" width)
1 11' piece of 1×14 (ripped at yard to 12" width)
1 6' piece of 1×2
3 12' pieces of 1×1
1 dozen of 6d finishing nails
1 pound of 5d finishing nails
⅛ pound of 2d brads
1½ dozen 2½" No. 8 wood screws
2 1½" button tip butt hinges and screws to match drawer pull
1 pull

Tools Needed

Crosscut saw	Rule
Rip saw	Drill and ⅛" bit
Keyhole saw	Nail set
Hammer	Countersink
Block plane	Chisel and mallet
Screwdriver	(to inset hinges)
Square	

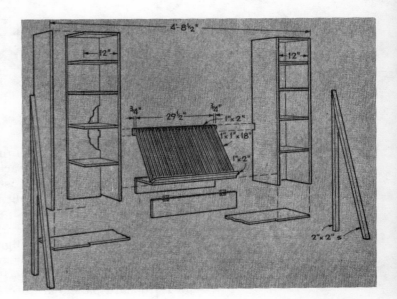

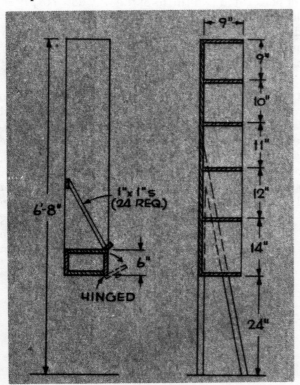

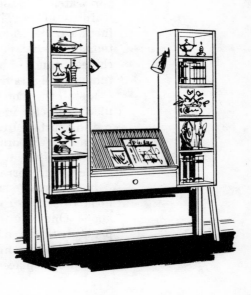

8
Turning Wasted Walls into Working Walls

The "good life" has given us more possessions, along with the problem of where to store them. One practical solution is to utilize every inch of wall space in your storage area by installing perforated hardboard paneling. It gets equipment off the floors, out of corners, and onto walls—where it is always close at hand.

You can make working walls with perforated hardboard panels, for while they are sturdy, they are light enough to install single-handed. It takes no special skills to cut, saw, or mount these panels; standard woodworking tools are all you need.

Hardboard panels are a durable, low-maintenance product; they have no grain to split, check, craze, or raise, and they have no knots to spoil the appearance or weaken the panel. They're stable and have excellent strength properties in all directions with no unequal stresses. Their rugged, hard surface resists denting, scratching, marring, and wear.

Pegboard panels come with even or random V-grooved planking either fully perforated from top to bottom or perforated two-thirds of the way down to give a wainscot effect. They come factory-finished in colors or patterns that need no further treatment or in a hard-surface neutral tan or brown finish, standard or tempered, that is ready to spray, brush, or roller paint in the color of your choice. Standard hardboard panels are generally 4' x 8' x ¼", but you can get them in heights from 4' to 16' if you wish.

Install them on studs or furring strips with adhesive, nails, or screws. When placed directly on solid walls, ¼" spacers should be used between the panel and nailing surface to allow clearance for hanger fixtures. Available hooks, brackets, and heavy-duty hardware support all manner of items from small tools to heavy equipment (ladders, lawn mowers, automobile parts and spare tires, garden gear, terrace furniture, etc.).

If you have no basement space for a workshop, you can even eke out a corner nook to set up counters and shelves with your tools hanging conveniently above. One way to keep tools in their accustomed places is to use a marking pencil or tape to outline their shapes right on the board. (Then lay down a firm rule to those members of the family with "takings ways" to put them back in their proper places.)

Perforated hardboard panels and hanging hardware and brackets are available from your local lumber or building-supply dealer. All you need to do now to get your storage room or garage out of the "catchall" junk status is to use some of these sketched ideas to turn wasted space into working walls.

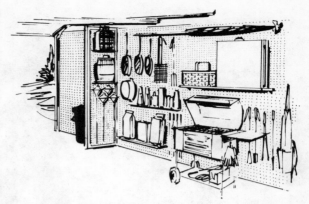

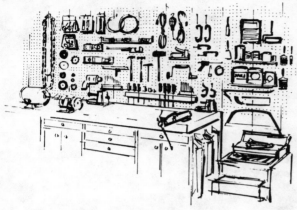

No basement workshop in your home? How about using a corner of a spare room to set up counterspace, cabinets, and a place for all the precious tools you need to do major and minor household repairs? With perforated walls, it makes a place for everything—and right at your fingertips.

Won't memories of your barbecues linger longer if you're assured that all the wherebys can be stacked away on shelves and walls when the fun is over? Note, too, the extension panel that hides it all from outdoor view and makes a good spot for storing refuse cans.

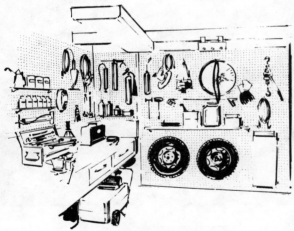

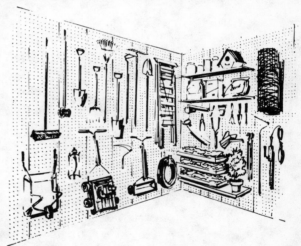

How much time do you spend over the weekend hunting up missing automobile parts for minor repairs, tinkering, washing, or polishing your car? You can at least cut down the search and make it easier for yourself by keeping needed equipment in full view and ready to use.

Wouldn't it be nice each spring, summer, and autumn when you have to keep up with garden chores to have all your working paraphernalia neatly hanging at hand on a perforated hardboard wall? It's one way, too, to be able to drive into the garage without climbing out of your car to pick up the equipment lying about the floor.

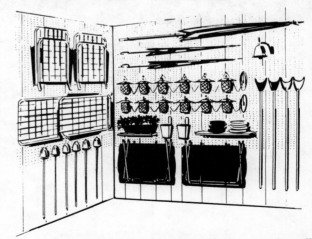

Come late autumn, wouldn't you like to hand up all the garden gear and terrace furniture and accessories where they will be out of the way? Try using a hardboard wall liner perforated to the wainscot level.

9
Sleepy Stairs Storage Wall

Here is a combination sleep, play, and storage area that will delight the younger child. Climbing up the "sleepy stairs" makes bedtime seem like fun (at least for a while). By putting all these activities together, the child gets a real feeling of having a place all his own.

One side of the platform is a raised built-in bed; the other side is a play area with shelves for toys and games. The stairs not only give the toddler his first practice at stair climbing, but they also provide additional storage area for his favorite things in the form of pull-out drawers. There is room for "vehicles" and other larger toys underneath.

The back wall of this project is made of perforated hardboard. Birch plywood, framing materials, and a little bit of hardware are the basics. Add a mattress, some light gay paint, and a little imaginative decoration. Then watch your child's eyes light up.

Materials List

    3 sheets of ¾" birch plywood
    1 sheet of ¼" birch plywood (for back and drawer bottom)
    10' of 1½ × 2 birch (for bottom bed rail)
    60' of 1¼ × 1¼ birch (for rail spindles)
    26' of 1½ × 1½ birch (for hand rail)
    12' of ¾ × 2 birch (for shelf facer)
    3' of ¾ × 2 birch (for top shelf facer)
    40' of ⅝ × 1⅞ birch (for blocks on rail spindles)
    30' of 1 × 4 lumber (for drawer guides)
    3 sheets of ⅛" perforated hardboard
    76' of 1 × 3 lumber (for framing perforated hardboard wall)

Hardware
1½' linear feet of 1½" piano hinge and screws.

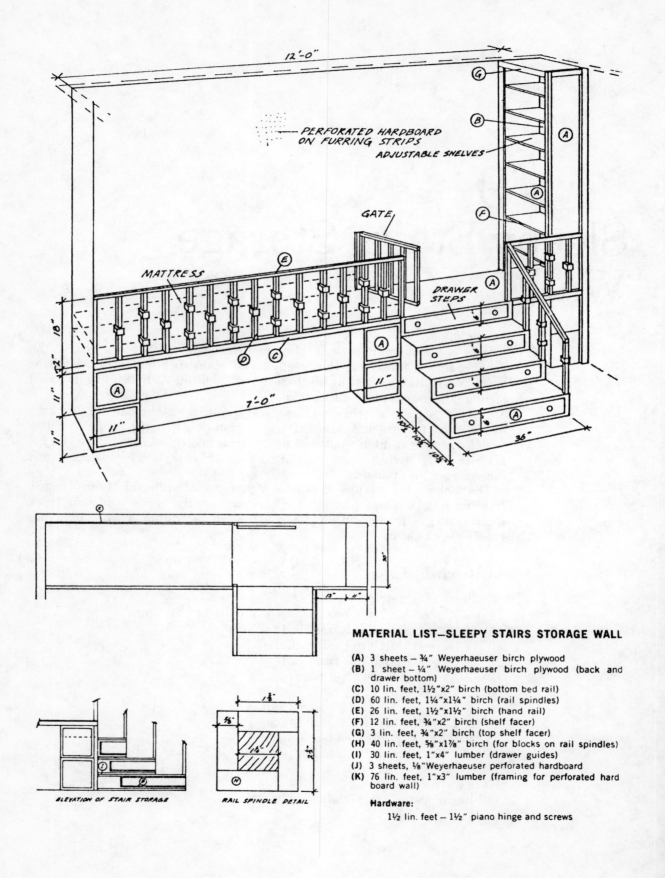

PERFORATED HARDBOARD ON FURRING STRIPS

ADJUSTABLE SHELVES

GATE

MATTRESS

DRAWER STEPS

12'-0"

7'-0"

ELEVATION OF STAIR STORAGE

RAIL SPINDLE DETAIL

MATERIAL LIST—SLEEPY STAIRS STORAGE WALL

(A) 3 sheets — ¾" Weyerhaeuser birch plywood
(B) 1 sheet — ¼" Weyerhaeuser birch plywood (back and drawer bottom)
(C) 10 lin. feet, 1½"x2" birch (bottom bed rail)
(D) 60 lin. feet, 1¼"x1¼" birch (rail spindles)
(E) 26 lin. feet, 1½"x1½" birch (hand rail)
(F) 12 lin. feet, ¾"x2" birch (shelf facer)
(G) 3 lin. feet, ¾"x2" birch (top shelf facer)
(H) 40 lin. feet, ⅝"x1⅞" birch (for blocks on rail spindles)
(I) 30 lin. feet, 1"x4" lumber (drawer guides)
(J) 3 sheets, ⅛"Weyerhaeuser perforated hardboard
(K) 76 lin. feet, 1"x3" lumber (framing for perforated hard board wall)

Hardware:

1½ lin. feet — 1½" piano hinge and screws

10
Portable Built-in Wall

This portable built-in wall may be just the answer for the space and storage problems in your home or apartment. Designed by Franklyn Jacoby, A.S.I.D., the units stack one on top of another, are completely interchangeable, and can be moved easily. This new concept in a storage wall houses the television, stereo, records, books, games, hobbies, and collections. This one is built of redwood, redwood plywood, and overlaid plywood that requires no painting or finishing. The selection of hinges and hardware helps set the built-in style, and the available designs allow for a wide choice from modern to traditional styling.

Before starting construction on your project, it is helpful to work out the actual dimensions on the plans and exploded drawings shown here. Allow for the thickness of the plywood and the redwood, noting that the plywood is a full thickness of ¾″, but that the 1″ redwood is a net of ¾″. Do not plan to build the cabinets to the ceiling; if you leave approximately 4″ to 6″ at the top, the space will be concealed by the valance.

No specific dimensions have been given since exact sizes will vary according to individual needs. Those shown on the plan are approximate sizes that can be adjusted for any room. When a move is necessitated, additional modular units can be added for a larger room. The units also can be stacked back-to-back to create a most-interesting room divider.

The base of this wall unit is made of ¾″ black high-density overlaid plywood.

The doors and sides of the lower units are made of ¾″ redwood plywood, the tops and bottoms are made of ¾″ black high-density overlaid plywood, and the backs and shelves are made of ¼″ white acrylic overlaid plywood.

The top units are made of 1 × 10, certified kiln-dried, clear, all-heart California redwood with ¼″ white acrylic overlaid plywood backs and shelves. This lumber can also be used for the shelving in the upper units.

The storage cabinets and speakers were built of this same material, with redwood plywood used for the cabinet doors.

All of the units can be constructed using simple box construction with butt joints. Use glue and screws for maximum strength. For the best appearance, fasten the countertop to the lower units with a spline joint or with angle braces or blocking screwed from the inside into the material. Since the top units stack

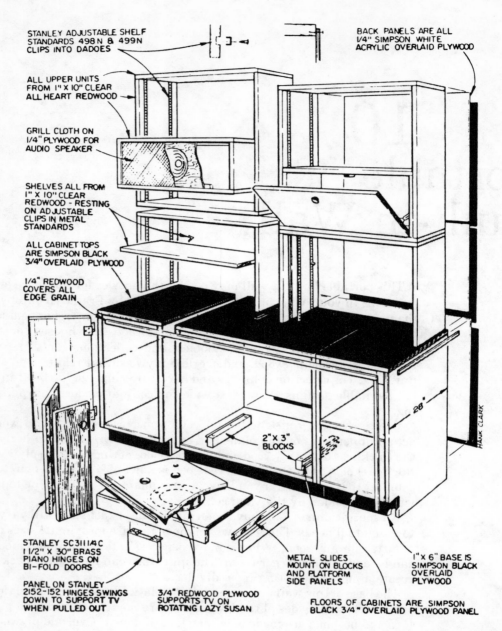

STANLEY ADJUSTABLE SHELF
STANDARDS 498N & 499N
CLIPS INTO DADOES

BACK PANELS ARE ALL
1/4" SIMPSON WHITE
ACRYLIC OVERLAID PLYWOOD

ALL UPPER UNITS
FROM 1" X 10" CLEAR
ALL HEART REDWOOD

GRILL CLOTH ON
1/4" PLYWOOD FOR
AUDIO SPEAKER

SHELVES ALL FROM
1" X 10" CLEAR
REDWOOD - RESTING
ON ADJUSTABLE
CLIPS IN METAL
STANDARDS

ALL CABINET TOPS
ARE SIMPSON BLACK
3/4" OVERLAID PLYWOOD

1/4" REDWOOD
COVERS ALL
EDGE GRAIN

28"

HANK CLARK

2" X 3"
BLOCKS

STANLEY SC 31114 C
1 1/2" X 30" BRASS
PIANO HINGES ON
BI-FOLD DOORS

PANEL ON STANLEY
2152-152 HINGES SWINGS
DOWN TO SUPPORT TV
WHEN PULLED OUT

3/4" REDWOOD PLYWOOD
SUPPORTS TV ON
ROTATING LAZY SUSAN

METAL SLIDES
MOUNT ON BLOCKS
AND PLATFORM
SIDE PANELS

FLOORS OF CABINETS ARE SIMPSON
BLACK 3/4" OVERLAID PLYWOOD PANEL

1" X 6" BASE IS
SIMPSON BLACK
OVERLAID
PLYWOOD

on top of each other, the screws are concealed.

To assemble the units, place the base units on the floor and level them. The weight of the larger lower units holds them in place. You may wish to drill through the units and bolt together with 1¾" or 2" bolts to ensure a level countertop. The hutch units then can be placed in position. Since the speakers and cabinets are completely interchangeable within the top units, they can be placed wherever desired. The

finished look is achieved using ¼ × ¾, certified kiln-dried, clear, all-heart California redwood to cover all of the edge grain of the plywood units and shelves.

Use adjustable shelf standards and clips to make the shelves completely flexible.

Close-up full-front views of the two sections show how each could stand alone as a project. Small locks are an option for the large cabinet doors. Using this concept, the entire wall need not be built at once. For example, a homeowner may wish to build only a cabinet for the stereo or television and to add other units later.

Television Unit

The exploded drawing shows how units are tied together. The detail shows the assembly of a shelf for a television set. This allows the set to be completely usable wherever the unit is placed. It can be pulled out from the cabinet and swiveled in any direction free of the sides. To allow for proper ventilation, large holes should be drilled in the back and bottom of the unit housing the television. For additional support and counterbalance of weight, it is advisable to use large eye screws and wire to secure this unit to the floor.

Interchangeable Cabinet Construction

The detailed drawing shows typical construction of one of the interchangeable cabinets. These can be designed with doors as shown or with a drop door. The inside can be designed with a partition or shelving, or it can be left completely open.

Lighting and Wiring

Complete flexibility is designed into the lighting and wiring system. All wires are concealed either behind the backs of the units or the valance. Small holes drilled in the backs of the units facilitate the wiring of speakers and

stereo components, the television antenna and controls, and lighting control. The valance is the only part of this project that must in any way be fixed to a wall or ceiling.

The nerve center for the lighting and television is centered on two items on the shelves. On a bottom shelf is an automatic tenn-a-liner antenna rotor, which controls the crossfire antenna for the television set. On the shelf above are two electronic dimmer controls built into a redwood box (see lighting fixture detail). These dimmers, which control the lighting intensity to create virtually any mood desired, are wired so that the box plugs directly into a standard 110-volt house circuit.

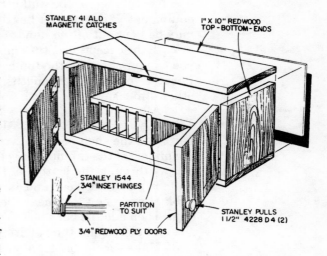

STANLEY 41 ALD MAGNETIC CATCHES
1" X 10" REDWOOD TOP - BOTTOM - ENDS
STANLEY 1544 3/4" INSET HINGES
PARTITION TO SUIT
3/4" REDWOOD PLY DOORS
STANLEY PULLS 1 1/2" 4228 D 4 (2)

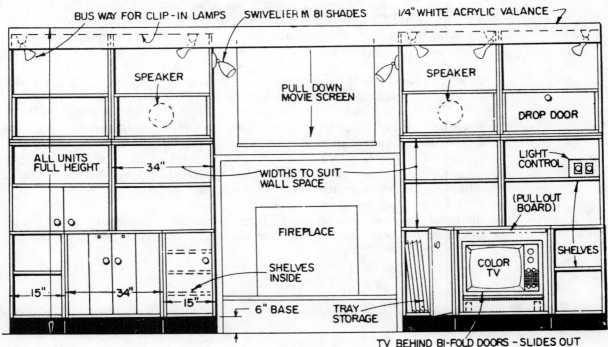

BUS WAY FOR CLIP-IN LAMPS
SWIVELIER M 81 SHADES
1/4" WHITE ACRYLIC VALANCE
SPEAKER
PULL DOWN MOVIE SCREEN
SPEAKER
DROP DOOR
ALL UNITS FULL HEIGHT
34"
WIDTHS TO SUIT WALL SPACE
LIGHT CONTROL
(PULLOUT BOARD)
FIREPLACE
SHELVES
15"
34"
15"
SHELVES INSIDE
COLOR TV
6" BASE
TRAY STORAGE
TV BEHIND BI-FOLD DOORS - SLIDES OUT

11
Wall Cabinets for Tools

A tool cabinet for the wall behind your workbench provides a handy place for equipment. If the cabinet has doors and a lock, sharp-edged or expensive tools may be kept out of the hands of small children.

With the exception of the ends, which are cut back to accommodate the doors, you can purchase all the lumber in the indicated widths so that you need only to cut it to the proper lengths. The top and bottom pieces are 67¾" long. All other dimensions are shown on the drawing.

1. After cutting the pieces to size, fasten the two ends, A and B, to the bottom board using No. 6, 1¾" long wood screws. Holes should be countersunk. Next add the shelf board and the top. Then insert the large partition piece in the middle of the cabinet between the shelf and the top board, fastening it with screws through the bottom of the shelf and through the top board. Insert the bottom partition piece and fasten it with screws through the bottom of the cabinet and one screw near the front edge of the shelf.

2. Then add the back boards to the assembly, fastening them with screws to the end pieces and the partition boards.

3. Make each door of 3 pieces of lumber 11½" wide. Hold the pieces together with a cleat 11½" wide and a piece of 2 × 4. The 2 × 4, in addition to serving as a cleat, should provide space for storage of drills, auger bits, punches, etc. A series of holes bored into the upper edge of the 2 × 4 will accommodate these small tools.

4. Fasten the doors to the cabinet with 3" hinges, recessed into both the doors and the sides of the cabinet to the thickness of 1 hinge leaf. Mark the position of each hinge carefully before chiseling out the recess.

5. The cabinet may be placed on the workbench. But for added working space and ease of opening the doors when material is on the bench, place 1' or 2' above the bench. Fasten it to the wall with 4 lag screws placed near the 4 inside corners of the cabinet. First bore ⅜" holes in the boards for the lag screws; place the cabinet on a box or have someone hold it to the desired height while you mark the position of the holes on the wall.

6. For a brick, concrete, or cinder block wall, the holes (2" deep and ½" in diameter) may be made with a carbide tip bit and power drill or with a star drill and hammer. Insert expansion shields in the holes and draw the lag

screws up tightly with a wrench.

7. Add brackets, hooks, and other fasteners as needed to accommodate your equipment.

One for All Your Hand Tools

This tool cabinet was designed to hold virtually the complete Stanley line of carpenter's tools. Note the convenient rack for storing chisels, drill bits, punches, etc. There is ample space for almost any hand tool the woodworker may need.

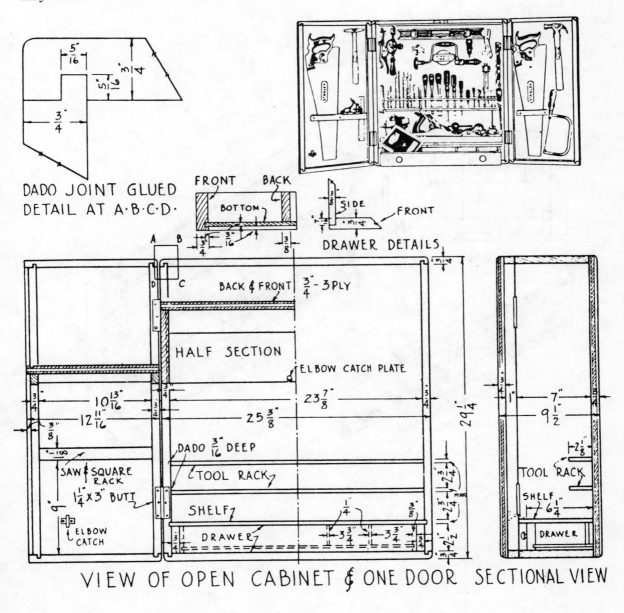

DADO JOINT GLUED DETAIL AT A·B·C·D·

DRAWER DETAILS

VIEW OF OPEN CABINET & ONE DOOR   SECTIONAL VIEW

Materials List

6 pieces, ¾″ × 12″ × 2½′
2 pieces, ¾″ × 12″ × 2′6½″
1 piece, ¾″ × 7″ × 5′7¾″
1 piece, ¾″ × 7″ × 2′4⁵/₁₆″
5 pieces, ¾″ × 8″ × 5′8¼″
1 piece, ¾″ × 8″ × 6⅝″
2 pieces, ¾″ × 8″ × 5′7¾″
2 pieces, ¾″ × 8″ × 3′1¼″
No. 6, 1¾″ wood screws
4 3″ hinges
⅜″ × 3″ lag screws
Assorted hardware for tools

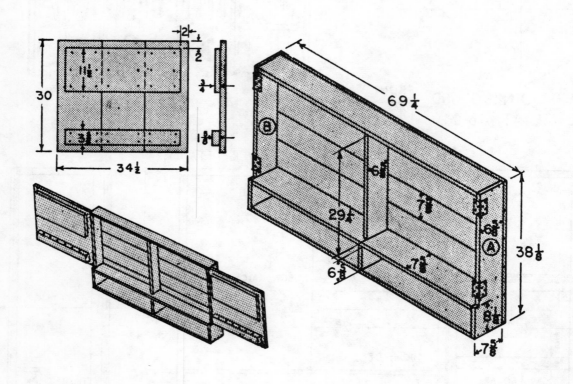

12
Grow-along Desk

This convertible table desk, 23¾″ high for the use of the small child, may be transformed to a full desk height of 28″ when the child grows up.

The tabletop is made of three boards held together with ⅜″ dowels and glue. Use six 4″ dowel lengths in each matching edge. Bore the dowel holes 2¼″ deep, using a doweling jig to assure perfect alignment. Clamp the assembly together until the glue has set. Hardwood plywood may also be used for the top.

The base sections are made of 1 × 12 lumber, fastened together with glue and 6d finishing nails. The large panels forming the sides of the bases may be edge-glued, if desired.

To make the low desk, place the base sections with the opening downward. To make the high desk, place the bases as shown in the large drawing, thus providing shelf space. Fasten the top to the bases with 3 corner braces, evenly spaced on each side of each base. The corner braces are fastened with wood screws, which are easily detached for raising or lowering the height of the desk.

Sand the desk, rounding all sharp edges. Finish by staining and varnishing to accentuate the beauty of the wood.

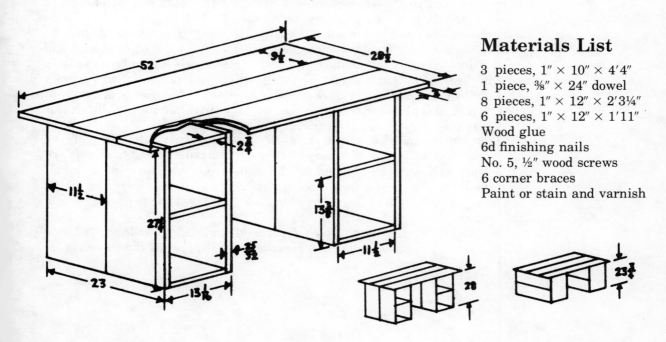

Materials List

3 pieces, 1″ × 10″ × 4′4″
1 piece, ⅜″ × 24″ dowel
8 pieces, 1″ × 12″ × 2′3¼″
6 pieces, 1″ × 12″ × 1′11″
Wood glue
6d finishing nails
No. 5, ½″ wood screws
6 corner braces
Paint or stain and varnish

13
Portable Shelving—Put It Where You Need It

Shelving for the basement, garage, or storage room usually is anchored to a wall or at least to the overhead joists. Sturdy shelves can be provided, however, without such permanent fastenings. A self-locking ladder and shelf arrangement makes possible the transfer of shelves from one place to another with a minimum of effort.

The shelf structure consists simply of a series of ladders, built of 2 × 4's with double rungs. The space between the rungs is a wide slot, into which cleats, attached to the underside of the shelves, fit snugly to lock the entire structure together.

First make six 2 × 4 ladder rails, each 6′ long. Make sure that the foot of each rail is perfectly square so that it will sit flat on the floor—in fact, so square that it can stand by itself. Then from this perfectly square end, measure up exactly 8″ on each rail, and use a square to draw a straight line across the small sides of the 2 × 4. Repeat the process at 28″, at 48″, and at 68″. These lines show the placement of the top of the rungs.

Then nail the rungs, pieces of 1 × 4, 22″ long, to the rails with 8d common nails, 2 to each point. When completed, the ladders should be true enough to stand by themselves on a perfectly flat surface.

Each shelf consists of three 1 × 6 boards, 10′ long. Here again, square the ends of each board. Then measure back 4 inches from the squared end and draw a line across the face of the board. For any one-shelf assembly, these lines on the three-shelf board should line up evenly; the cleat is nailed perfectly straight by using the line to mark the placement of the outer edge of the cleat. The next cleat is placed in the same manner 58″ from the end. The third cleat is similarly placed 4″ from the other end of the shelf assembly.

When nailing the cleats, it is easier to place them by nailing through the cleat into the shelf board. This may be done with 3d nails. When the cleats are placed properly on a shelf assembly, 5d nails are driven through the shelf board and the cleat and are clinched beneath.

The completed shelf is then set in place, so that the 3 cleats fit snugly into the 3 slots.

The structure calls for the use of three ladders. A two-ladder job has a tendency to sway, unless diagonal cross-bracing is used. In the three-ladder structure there is no sway. If the job is not done carefully, it may be necessary to drive small wedges beneath the cleats and the rungs.

Materials List

6 pieces, 2″ × 4″ × 6′
12 pieces, 1″ × 6″ × 10′
24 pieces, 1″ × 4″ × 1′10″
12 pieces, 1″ × 4″ × 1′5½″
96 8d common nails
3d and 5d nails for cleats

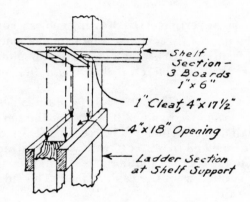

Shelf Section— 3 Boards 1″ x 6″

1″ Cleat, 4″x 17½″

4″x 18″ Opening

Ladder Section at Shelf Support

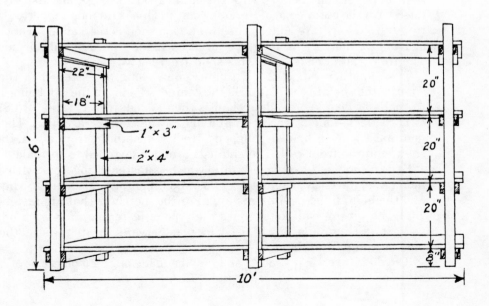

22″
18″
6′
1″x 3″
2″x 4″
10′
20″
20″
20″
8″

14
Built-in Wall Cabinet

The lower-right portion of the drawing shows a cutaway section exposing the frame for the floor of this cabinet. The frame is made of 2 × 4's (2 pieces 68½″ long for the front and back, and 2 pieces 6¾″ long for the ends). The rear 2 × 4 is fastened to the wall before the floor board, 9½″ × 68½″ × 1″ is nailed to the frame.

Two pieces cut to 9½″ × 65¼″ × 1″ form the sides of the cabinet. These are first cut out, as shown, to a width of 7½″ for the top 30″ of their length, so that the upper half of the cabinet will be recessed. The sides are then fastened to the 2 × 4 base frame and to a 2″ × 3″ rail which is attached to the wall flush with the top of the side boards. Another 2″ × 3″ rail is fastened to the wall, so that its upper edge is 30⅞″ from the cabinet floor. The side boards are nailed also to this middle rail.

The top of the cabinet, 1″ × 7½″ × 70″ is then nailed to the top rail and to the side boards, thus completing a firm overall frame for the cabinet.

Another rail of 2 × 3 lumber, 68½″ long is suspended from the side boards so that its upper edge is flush with the cutaway shelf ledge, and its outer edge is flush with the outer edge of the side boards. This is further supported when the three "front legs" are added. The lower open shelf is then added. This is a piece of 1 × 11½ lumber, 70″ long cut out at each end to fit around the side boards. The front rail is fastened to this shelf from below.

Then another rail of 2 × 3 lumber, 68½″ long, is fastened to the wall to support the shelf in the bottom of the cabinet, the top of the rail being 18″ above the cabinet floor. The middle shelf is then added; it is 1″ × 9½″ × 68½″.

Three legs—one at each end and one in the center—are next. These are of nominal 1 × 3 stock, 35¼″ long, and are fastened to the front 2 × 4, the middle shelf, and the front rail. The end legs are also fastened to the side boards.

Except for the 2 × 4 base frame, which is fastened together with 16d common nails, the entire cabinet uses 6d or 8d finishing nails, with the heads sunk and the holes filled before finishing. For the members that are fastened to the wall, the type of wall determines the type of fastening. For brick or concrete walls, blunt cut nails may be used; for plaster walls, locate the studs behind the plaster and nail to them.

The doors are 15¼″ × 30½″ and may be made of glued pieces or of hardwood plywood.

Materials List

2 pieces, $2'' \times 4'' \times 5'8\frac{1}{2}''$
2 pieces, $2'' \times 4'' \times 6\frac{3}{4}''$
1 piece, $1'' \times 10'' \times 5'8\frac{1}{2}''$
2 pieces, $1'' \times 10'' \times 5'5\frac{1}{4}''$
4 pieces, $2'' \times 3'' \times 5'8\frac{1}{2}''$
1 piece, $1'' \times 12'' \times 5'10''$
1 piece, $1'' \times 10'' \times 5'8\frac{1}{2}''$
3 pieces, $1'' \times 3'' \times 2'11\frac{1}{4}''$
2 pieces, $1'' \times 8'' \times 5'8\frac{1}{2}''$
1 piece, $1'' \times 8'' \times 5'10''$
1 piece, $1'' \times 8'' \times 2'6''$
2 pieces, $5'' \times 2'7'' \times 1''$
4 pieces, $15\frac{1}{4}'' \times 30\frac{1}{2}'' \times \frac{3}{4}''$ hardwood plywood or glued pieces of $\frac{3}{4}'' \times 8''$ planed to size
16d common nails
6d or 8d finishing nails
8 hinges
Door knobs or pulls
Paint, or stain and varnish

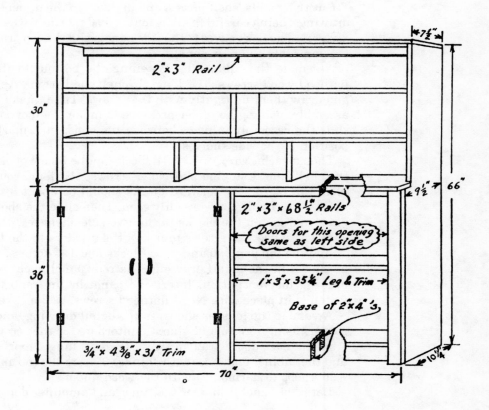

15
Amplifier–Record Cabinet

The cabinet shown here provides for the amplifier in the lower section, the tuner in the center, and the record player in the top section. The two side sections are used for storage of record albums. Doors protect the equipment and add beauty to the finished cabinet.

Top, end, and door panels may be of edge-glued ¾" lumber, or they may be of hardwood plywood. The back panel is of ¼" hardwood plywood. Shelves, dividers, and legs are of ¾" lumber.

Cut the panels, shelf pieces, and dividers to the dimensions indicated on the drawings, being careful to allow for the ³⁄₁₆" mortises where the shelves join the dividers. The back edges of the side panels and the top are rabbetted ¼" × ¼" to accommodate the rear panel.

Assemble the cabinet by fastening the bottom to the ends, using No. 4 flathead wood screws, 1½" long, through the bottom. Apply glue to the joints and draw them up tightly with the screws. Then, make the shelf and divider assembly, using glue under pressure to make the mortise joints. Temporarily slide the assembly in place between the ends; then mark off on each end the position of the side shelves.

Then attach two ¾" × ¾" × 4" blocks on the inside of each end panel beneath the shelf line. Use glue and No. 4 screws, 1¼" long, countersunk to hold the blocks in place. The forward blocks should be about 3" from the front of the shelf so they will not be readily seen. Then slide the shelf assembly back into place and fasten the blocks to the two side shelves with 1¼" screws, counter sunk. Also use 1½" screws to fasten the dividers to the bottom.

Add the top panel, using wood blocks and 1¼" screws, as for the shelves and as shown in the detail drawing. The rear panel is cut to provide a 17" × 17" opening for ventilation. Insert the panel in the rabbeted rear opening and fasten it in place with No. 3 flathead screws, ¾" long, set about 6" apart.

Assemble the legs, as shown in the detail drawing, and attach them at each corner, using screws and glue. Counterbore for the screws.

Mount each door with two 1½" × 1½" butt hinges mortised into the door edge and the cabinet end. Locate the hinges 3" from the top and bottom of the doors. Add knobs to harmonize with the wood finish.

Detail of panel fronts for the tuner and amplifier depends upon the location of the control knobs. These panels are ¼″ lumber or hardwood plywood and may be mounted on ¼″ × ½″ strips set in ½″ from the front edge of the openings. Use small screws or ornamental brass nails to hold the panels in place.

Mount the record player on roller drawers to facilitate loading and unloading the player. Most hi-fi sets utilize separate speakers located in the room for best tone delivery; hence no provision is made in the cabinet for a speaker. However, if a speaker is to be included, increase the vertical dimensions of the cabinet to provide for an additional shelf.

Materials List

4 pieces, ¾″ × 9″ × 2′9″
8 pieces, ¾″ × 9″ × 2′10⅛″
4 pieces, ¾″ × 9″ × 1′6″
2 pieces, ¾″ × 7″ × 1′5″
2 pieces, ¾″ × 8″ × 2′10¹³⁄₃₆″
1 piece, ¾″ × ¾″ × 2′8″
1 piece, 2″ × 2″ × 3′4″
1 piece, ¼ × 32⅛″ × 34⅛″ hardwood plywood
2 pieces, ¾ × 16″ × 35″ or 2 pieces,
    ¾″ × 9″ × 2′10¹³⁄₃₆″
4 1½″ × 1½″ butt hinges
No. 4, 1½″ flathead screws
No. 4, 1¼″ flathead screws
No. 3, ¾″ flathead screws
Door knobs
Wood glue
(Additional paneling and details for front end depend upon the location for control knobs of units.)

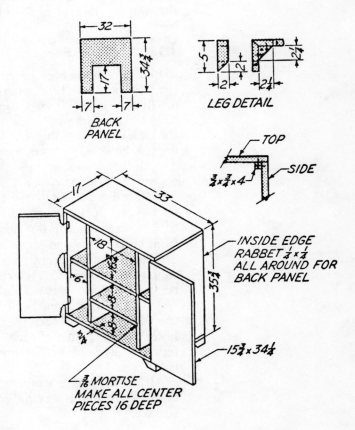

16
Super Workbench

If you want a workbench you'll be proud to show off to your friends, start planning to make this one now. It takes care and good workmanship, but you'll have a bench that is both well-designed and built to withstand years of hard use.

Before beginning, study the drawings. Although the plans may look complicated, they become quite clear when you break them into steps. Read once through all the instructions before starting.

Instructions

1. To make the back panel, cut three 46½" lengths of 1 × 6. Cleats consist of two 15¾" and one 16½" lengths of 1 × 2. Right cleat (16½" piece) and left cleat are flush to edge of panel. Right edge of middle cleat is 14¼" from right edge of panel. Fix cleats to 1 × 6's with glue and screws. Drill three 5/16" guide holes through each cleat into 1 × 6's. Position the holes off-center vertically. Countersink holes. Clean surfaces, apply glue, screw cleats to boards with No. 10, 1¼", flathead wood screws. (Whenever glue and screws are required in cleats, repeat these instructions.)

2. Cut five 26" lengths of 1 × 6" for left panel. Cleats of 1 × 2 stock are 25¼" for top and 26¾" for bottom. Runner fixed to bottom cleat is a 26¾" length of ½ × ½. Front end to top cleat gets a cut 1⅝" long and ¾" deep to receive top front brace. Glue and screw cleats to 1 × 6's, as before. Leave ¾" between butt ends of cleats and front panel edge. Top cleat is flush with panel top; bottom edge of lower cleat is 7⅞" from panel bottom. Drawer runner is fixed ½" from the top of lower cleat with glue and No. 4, 1½" long flathead wood screws.

3. Cut two 36" lengths of 5/4 × 8 for legs. The keys to cutting are these: (1) the outside edge of each leg is the natural straight edge of the 5/4 × 8, (2) the lower outside corner of each leg lines up with the vertical edge of the panel, (3) legs meet at dead center on the panel, and (4) distance from top of panel to floor is 32".

Attach the legs to the panel with glue and three ¼" bolts, 2½" long. Space ¼" holes evenly along legs and countersink them to bring bolt heads flush with leg surface.

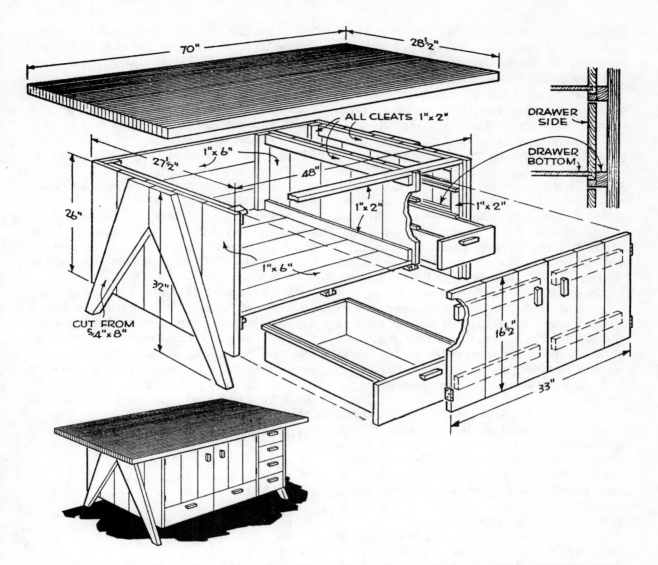

4. For the right panel, cut another five 26″ lengths of 1 × 6. Top cleat is a 23⅝″ length of 1 × 2, attached 1½″ from left side of panel, flush to top. Right cleat is a 25¼″ length that fits snugly against top cleat, flush to bottom of panel (allowing ¾″ at top for top brace). Bottom cleat is 25⅛″ long, flush to bottom of panel, and butts right cleat. Attach cleats as before.

Now study the drawer runner assembly in the sectional detail. Notice, too, in the exploded version, that the last drawer must hang from—not rest on—runners. Begin by cutting the four runners from ½ × ½ stock, each 25⅝″ long. The first two supports for the runners are 1 × 1's, and the lower member is a 1 × 2, since it will carry two runners. All three supports are 23⅝″ long. The key to positioning them is this: allow 5½″ from top of panel to top of first runner, another 5½″ to top of second runner, and 5″ to top of third runner. Check your measurements: the distance between top of panel and bottom of third runner should be 16½″. Attach supports with glue and No. 4, 1½″, flathead wood screws. Do the same with runners. Be certain you countersink all guide holes for screws.

5. Cut and attach legs as you did for left panel.

6. Begin interior partition by cutting five 17⁷⁄₁₆″ lengths of 1 × 6. Notch outer boards as

follows: up from bottom outside corner 15/16″ and in ¾″; at the top a ¾″ deep cut 1⅝″ long, back ¾″ from the top outside corner.

Both top and bottom cleats are 25¼″ long. Top cleat, flush to top of panel, is notched ¾″ deep and 1⅝″ long to receive top brace. Butt ends of cleats are ¾″ from right edge of partition. Bottom edge of lower cleat is 1 1/16″ from panel bottom. Attach cleats, as before.

Now cut 46½″ length of 1 × 2 for top brace. Attach it with glue and No. 8, 1½″, flathead wood screws to right and left panel, as indicated. Before doing this, however, drill two holes in brace to receive screws for interior partition. This should be at points between 12¾″ and 13½″ from right end of brace. Now install interior partition with glue and No. 8 screws. Fix it to back panel and top brace.

Next, cut five 25⅜″ runners from ½ × ½ stock. Fix the first four from the top down at the same level as runners on the right side panel. Fix the fifth runner to bottom left side of interior partition, after completing step 7. Attach these runners with glue and No. 4, 1″ screws.

7. For bottom panel, cut five 33″ lengths of 1 × 6. Attach them to cleats, as shown, with glue and No. 8, 1½″ screws. Mount for center runners straddles the center line of bottom panel. It is a 25⅜″ length of 1 × 1; runners the same length of ½ × ½. Attach mount with glue and No. 4, 1½″ screws and the runners with glue and No. 4, 1″ screws.

8. Cut sides and backs of all drawers from ½″ stock, which must be routed to receive ⅜″ stock drawer bottoms. If you don't own a router, have it done at the lumberyard when you buy the wood.

The drawers must match the runners, so take all measurements for drawers from runners already installed. The depth of all three bottom drawer faces should be 9½″. The three smaller drawers to the right are 5½″ deep at the face but vary inside, so measure carefully. Drawer faces are cut from 1 stock.

Fashion all drawer and cabinet pulls from 1 × 1 stock. Bevel length slightly on both sides with a plane, and cut into 3″ lengths. Lips on the three bottom drawers are cut from ½ × ½ stock.

Assemble the sides and back of each drawer first. Use glue and 1″ No. 4 flathead wood screws. Glue routed areas and slide ⅜″ bottom panel into place. Tack tight with 2d brads. Now put on face with glue and No. 4, 1½″ screws and the pulls with glue and No. 8, 1½″ screws.

9. Cut six 16½″ lengths of 1 × 6 for cabinet doors, and cut four 14″ sections of 1 × 2 for cleats. Install two cleats per door, as indicated. Attach pulls, as with drawers. Mortise areas for hinges. Screw them tight.

10. Your final job is the tabletop. It's also the easiest, involving only a repetition of the same tasks. Cut 38 lengths of 1 × 2, 70″ long. Each lamination of 1 × 2's is done with glue and four No. 8, 1½″ screws. Countersink guide holes so that screw heads are slightly below the surface of the wood.

Attach the top to the table, after the glue has set, with more glue and right-angle braces fixed to the side panels and underside of the tabletop. Then screw up through the top brace into top. The tabletop should be flush with back panel, allowing a 1′ overhang in front. Overhang should be equidistant on right and left. Sand, fill screw-head holes, and finish all but tabletop, as desired.

Materials List

4 pieces, 1″ × 6″ × 12′
1 piece, 1″ × 6″ × 14′
1 piece, 1″ × 6″ × 9′
3 pieces, 1″ × 2″ × 9′
39 pieces, 1″ × 2″ × 6′
2 pieces, ½″ × ½″ × 12′
1 piece, ½″ × ½″ × 14′
1 piece, ½″ × ½″ × 5′
1 piece, 1″ × 1″ × 9′
1 piece, 5/4″ × 8″ × 12′
1 piece, 1″ × 10″ × 4′
2 pieces, ½″ × 10″ × 9′
2 pieces, ½″ × 6″ × 9′
4 doz. No. 10, 1¼″ flathead wood screws
15 doz. No. 8, 1½″ flathead wood screws
5 doz. No. 4, 1½″ flathead wood screws
2 doz. No. 4, 1″ flathead wood screws
2 doz. No. 4, ¾″ flathead wood screws
⅛ lb. 2d brads
1 doz. 2½″–¼″ bolts and nuts
6 2″ right-angle braces and screws
4 2½ × 2½ button-tip butt hinges and screws
Glue

17
Room Divider

The height of this room divider should depend upon the height of the room. The length varies to fit the opening into which it is to be placed.

First make the outside frame (the two sides, top, and bottom), fastening it together with 8d finishing nails. Then make the center column for the lower shelves, cutting a dado groove 3/16″ deep for each shelf. Add the lower shelves and center column. Fasten the shelves to the sides with 6d finishing nails. Then add the framing material around the bottom half.

The upper shelves are staggered so that they may be fastened at each end with 6d finishing nails. The upper shelf joints also may be dado joints, if desired.

Depending upon the placement of the divider, one side may be completely covered with display panels of hardwood plywood or with board paneling to match the woodwork of the room it faces. If the divider is placed between a kitchen and dining area, the upper half may be left open and the center may be used for serving.

Slide the completed divider into place and nail it securely with 10d finishing nails to one wall, ceiling and floor. In nailing to the wall and ceiling, drive the nails into studs and joists, if possible; or use toggle bolts in place of nails.

Set the heads of all nails and fill the holes with wood filler. After the divider has been sanded smooth, it should be given a finish to match other woodwork.

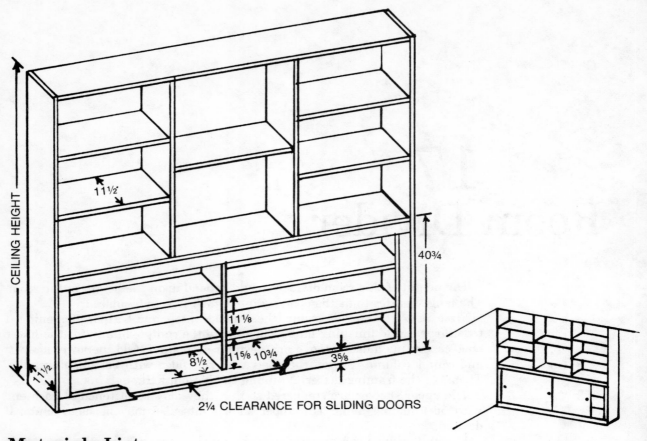

CEILING HEIGHT

11½

40¾

11⅛

11½

8½   11⅝ 10¾   3⅝

2¼ CLEARANCE FOR SLIDING DOORS

Materials List

1 × 12, 1 × 9, and 1 × 4 lumber.
(Dimensions depend on size of the room to be divided.)

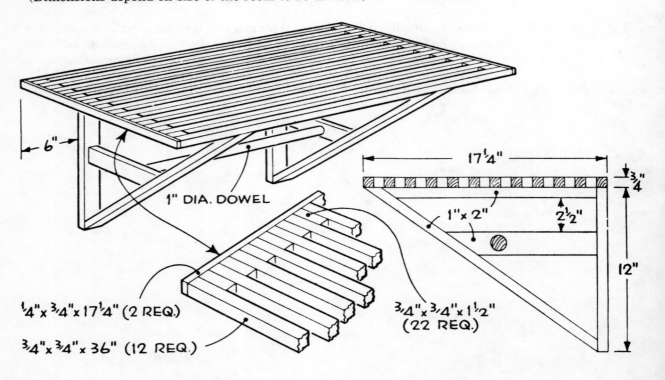

6"

1" DIA. DOWEL

17¼"

¾"

1"× 2"

2½"

12"

¼"× ¾"× 17¼" (2 REQ.)

¾"× ¾"× 36" (12 REQ.)

¾"× ¾"× 1½"
(22 REQ.)

18
Overhead Utility Rack

Here's a perfect overhead shelf for the utility room, where the family can store rain hats, gloves, and scarves. A sturdy clothes pole provides a place to hang coats, jackets, rainwear, or what-have-you. The slats allow wet gear to drain through onto the floor instead of becoming mildewed on the shelf.

Begin by making the shelf. Cut twelve 36″ lengths of ¾ × ¾ stock and 22 blocks 1½″ long. Cut the two end pieces 17¼″ long from ¼ × ¾ stock. Assemble the 36″ lengths and blocks first. Nail 3d finishing nails through the first blocks into the outer strip so that nail holes will be hidden from outer edge of shelf. Repeat until all twelve 36″ strips are in place. Then nail the end pieces in place with three 2d finishing nails or brads.

Start the frame by drawing the side view of the frame to scale on paper. Follow the dimensions shown in side view. Use a steel square to make accurate angles. This pattern serves as a guide for angle cuts in the frame.

Cut framing members from 1 × 2 stock. Before assembly, bore 1″ diameter holes half way through each center strut. Center of hole should measure 7″ from back edge of strut.

Nail 5d finishing nails through 12″ back support into top support and center strut. At this point, attach back support assembly to wall with screws and wall plugs or toggle bolts. With back and horizontal supports in place on the wall, nail diagonal supports in place with 5d finishing nails. Measure, cut, and nail 1″ diameter dowel into prebored half-deep holes.

Place shelf on frame, allowing an overhang of 6″ on either side, and nail in place over each support at 3 equidistant points with 3d finishing nails or brads. Set and fill nail holes, sand lightly, and finish rack.

Materials List

3 pieces, 12′ × ¾″ × ¾″   2′ of 1″ diameter dowel
1 piece, 3′ × ¾″ × ¾″   ¼-lb. 2d finishing nails
1 piece, 3′ × ⅓″ × ¾″   ¼-lb. 3d finishing nails
1 piece, 12′ 1″ × 2″   ¼-lb. 5d finishing nails

19
Built-in Magazine and Book Rack

This magazine and book rack is simple to construct and can be finished to match almost any decor. Furthermore, it is built primarily out of only two sheets of plywood, so the cost is comparatively low.

The sliding cabinets on the first level provide convenient storage for all kinds of materials, for records, or for anything else you'd like to hide away.

Study the drawings carefully, noting how each component matches with the cutting diagrams. Then follow the easy step-by-step instructions.

Instructions

1. First lay out the parts for the unit on two panels of plywood as shown in the cutting diagrams. (Note that one panel is ¾″ plywood and the other is ¼″ plywood.) Use a straightedge and large steel square, remembering to allow for saw kerfs as parts are laid out. Saw out the parts and true up the edges with 1/0 sandpaper wrapped around a block.

2. Rabbet the wall cabinet's top and bottom pieces for the end pieces. Then run dadoes for the sliding doors as shown in the detail. Install track at bottom. Assemble the cabinet without back, using glue and nails, seeing that all corners are square.

3. Cut the dog-leg-shaped brackets to support the sloping magazine shelf backs with a jigsaw or band saw. Position them upright on the shelves between 1 × 1 and beveled 2 × 2 blocking. Fasten the sloping shelf backs to these brackets with glue and brads. Then install quarter-round along the front edges of the shelves to hold magazines.

4. Nail 1 × 3 supports into the wall studs at height shown. Hang the cabinet in position on the wall, and nail into 1 × 3 supports through top and bottom of cabinet. The ¼″ plywood back paneling covers the 1 × 3 supports. Use adjustable metal shelf standards at stud locations to hold shelf brackets.

5. Fill nail holes, and after sanding, prime the cabinet and shelves with enamel undercoat. Sand again lightly, then apply at least two coats of top-grade semigloss enamel paint.

6. Cut the 2 × 3 stanchion, or post, just the right length to wedge between

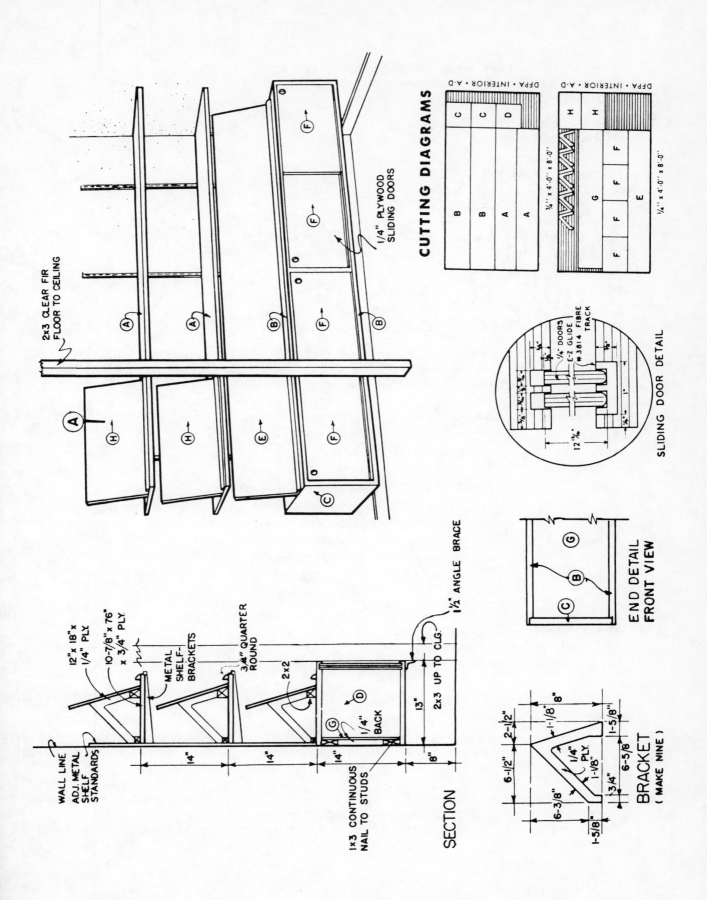

CUTTING DIAGRAMS

SLIDING DOOR DETAIL

END DETAIL FRONT VIEW

SECTION

BRACKET (MAKE NINE)

the floor and ceiling. After painting this post, position it and screw 1½″ angle braces to it at the right height for additional cabinet support.

Materials List
120
**Plywood (All Interior
Grade A-D, Good on One Side)**

Code	No.	Size	Use
A	2	10⅞″ × 76″	Shelf
B	2	13″ × 76″	Top and bottom
C	2	13″ × 13¼″	End
D	1	11¾″ × 12½″	Standard
E	1	12″ × 76″	Shelf back
F	4	12¹³/₁₆″ × 18¹³/₁₆″	Sliding doors
G	1	12½″ × 74½″	Back of unit
H	2	12″ × 18″	Shelf back
	9	(See drawing)	Brackets

Lumber and plywood

Amount	Size	Use
10½′	2″ × 2″	Back stop
10½′	1″ × 1″	Blocking for brackets
13′	1″ × 3″	Cabinet support
20′	¾ quarter round	Magazine support
1 piece (approximately)	8′ 2″ × 3″	Wood stanchion
16′	Adjustable	Metal standard
8 each	As required	Metal shelf brackets
1 each	1½″	Angle brace

Miscellaneous
4d and 6d finishing nails and brads
Glue and finishing materials

20
Three-way Sports Cabinet

This plywood unit serves as a camping–hiking cabinet or hunting–fishing cabinet or as storage for ski, golf, and tennis gear, as shown.

You can easily adapt it to other uses, too. Vary the shelves, racks, and drawers and you have efficient storage for canned goods, pots and pans, linens, or cleaning and laundry supplies. Or build a row of cabinets against the garage wall for tools, paints, and garden equipment.

CAMP, HIKE AND CLIMB CABINET

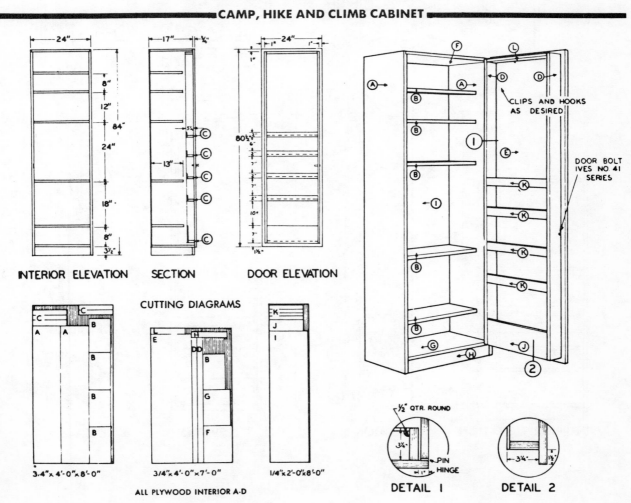

INTERIOR ELEVATION

SECTION

DOOR ELEVATION

CUTTING DIAGRAMS

3.4"x 4'-0"x8'-0"

3/4"x 4'-0"x7'-0"

1/4"x2'-0"x8'-0"

ALL PLYWOOD INTERIOR A-D

CLIPS AND HOOKS AS DESIRED

DOOR BOLT IVES NO. 41 SERIES

½" QTR. ROUND

PIN HINGE

DETAIL 1

DETAIL 2

HUNTING-FISHING CABINET

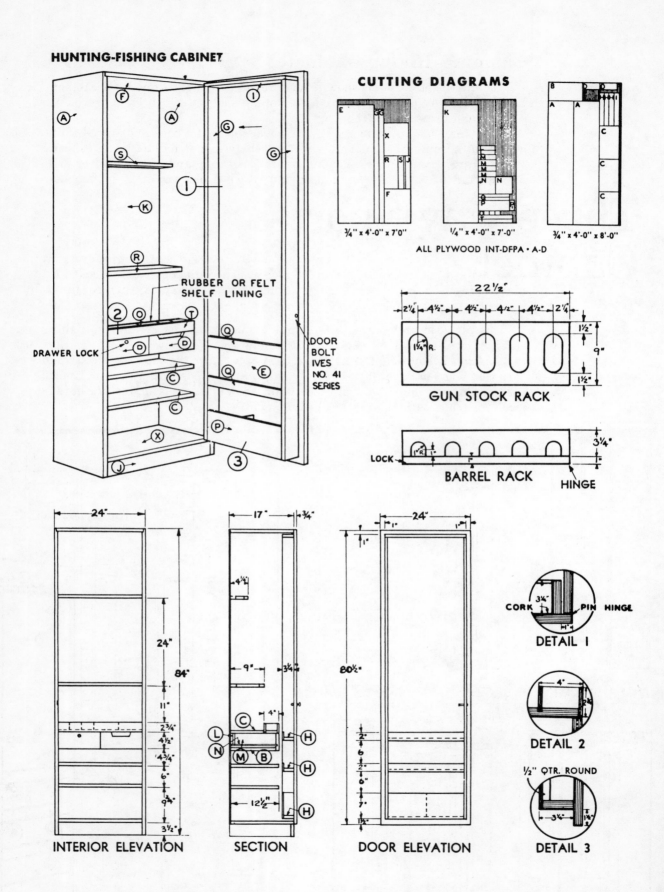

CUTTING DIAGRAMS

¾" x 4'-0" x 7'0"   ¼" x 4'-0" x 7'-0"   ¾" x 4'-0" x 8'-0"

ALL PLYWOOD INT-DFPA · A-D

RUBBER OR FELT SHELF LINING

DRAWER LOCK

DOOR BOLT IVES NO. 41 SERIES

22½"

GUN STOCK RACK

BARREL RACK

LOCK   HINGE

INTERIOR ELEVATION   SECTION   DOOR ELEVATION

CORK   PIN HINGE

DETAIL 1

DETAIL 2

½" QTR. ROUND

DETAIL 3

Camping–Hiking Cabinet

This and the other plans show several variations in the same basic cabinet. They all utilize the space-saving door-storage shelves, which have proven so popular and practical.

Cut, fit, and sand parts as required. Rabbet sides A for back and top. Glue all joints; nail through sides into top, base, and shelves; then nail back into rabbet.

Nail frame around door, allowing clearance shown, and install shelves and fascia. Finish completely, hang door, and attach hooks and other fittings desired.

Hunting–Fishing Cabinet

If you own hunting and fishing equipment, you will appreciate having a cabinet like this in which to keep your gear. The gun rack can be locked to prevent children from tampering with your guns. Fishing tackle can be stored in an organized manner so that anything you need is easy to find and ready for use.

Ski, Golf, and Tennis Cabinet

Anyone who has had skis, poles, golf clubs, and other long objects fall forward as he opens a closet door can appreciate one of the wrinkles in this plan.

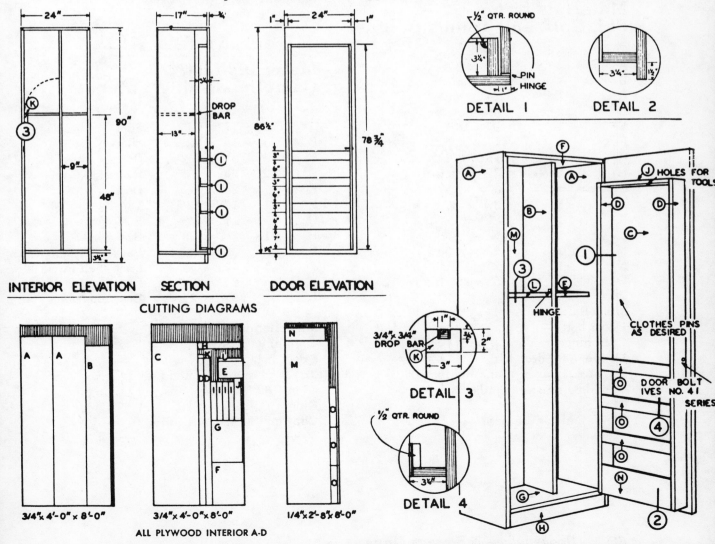

INTERIOR ELEVATION   SECTION   DOOR ELEVATION

CUTTING DIAGRAMS

3/4"x 4'-0" x 8'-0"   3/4"x 4'-0"x 8'-0"   1/4"x2'-8"x 8'-0"

ALL PLYWOOD INTERIOR A-D

DETAIL 1   DETAIL 2

DETAIL 3

DETAIL 4

The drop bar shown in Detail 3 guards against bruises and bumps by retaining tall articles in place.

Spring clothespins inside the door hold the small items that so often become wadded up in a shelf corner.

After studying these plans, take the job of building your three-way sports cabinet one step at a time. You can adapt the shelf arrangement shown to suit your equipment.

Instructions

1. First lay out the cabinet parts on three panels of plywood, as shown in the cutting diagrams. Use a straightedge and large steel square. Remember to allow for saw kerfs when laying out the parts.

2. Saw out parts and true up cut edges of the plywood with 1–0 sandpaper wrapped around a block. Rabbet one end of each side panel for the top.

3. Assemble the cabinet back-side down on the floor with resin glue and finishing nails. Square all corners. When the top, bottom, and back are in place, build shelves and drawers as shown in the drawings.

4. Make cutouts for gun stock and barrel racks, as shown in the detail. Glue and nail at heights to fit the guns you have. Install hinged bar with lock on barred rack.

5. Join the door framing strips on the door panel, allowing clearance all around as indicated. Then add shelves and facings. These facings should be flush with the frame. Lay cabinet with back down and install door, using 4 pin hinges.

6. Smooth all joints and slightly round all corners with 1/0 sandpaper.

7. Prime the cabinet with enamel undercoat. Sand lightly, and then give the cabinet at least two coats of top-grade semigloss enamel paint. Installing the door bolt and the lining as required finishes the job.

Materials List: Ski, Golf, and Tennis Cabinet

Code	No.	Size
A	2	17″ × 90″
B	1	13″ × 85″
C	1	24″ × 86½″
D	2	3¼″ × 78¾″
E	1	9″ × 13″
F	1	17″ × 23¼″
G	1	16¾″ × 22½″
H	1	3½″ × 22½″
I	4	3″ × 20½″
J	1	3¼″ × 20½″
K	1	2″ × 3″
L	1	¾″ × 12¾″
M	1	23¼″ × 86⅛″
N	1	7″ × 20½″
O	3	3″ × 20½″

Miscellaneous
1 door bolt
4 pin hinges
1¾ hinge for drop bar
2½′ of ½″ quarter-round nailing strip
4d and 6d finishing nails
Glue
Clothespins as required

Materials List: Camping–Hiking Cabinet

Code	No.	Size	Use
A	2	17″ × 84″	Side
B	5	13″ × 22½″	Shelves
C	5	3″ × 20½″	Door shelves
D	2	3¼″ × 78″	Door side frame
E	1	24″ × 80½″	Door
F	1	17″ × 23¼″	Top
G	1	17″ × 22½″	Bottom shelf
H	1	3½″ × 22½″	Base
I	1	23¼″ × 80⅛″	Back
J	1	7″ × 20½″	Door shelf fascia
K	4	2″ × 20½″	Door shelf fascia
L	1	3¼″ × 20⅛″	Door top frame

Miscellaneous
4 pin hinges
1 door bolt
2½′ of ½″ quarter-round nailing strip
4d and 6d finishing nails
Glue
Clips and hooks as required

Materials List:
Hunting–Fishing Cabinet

Code	No.	Size	Use
A	2	17″ × 84″	Side
B	1	12″ × 22½″	Drawer shelf
C	3	12½″ × 22½″	Shelf
D	2	4½″ × 11¼″	Drawer fronts
E	1	24″ × 80½″	Door
F	1	17″ × 23¼″	Top
G	2	3¼″ × 77¼″	Door frame
H	3	3″ × 20½″	Door shelf
I	1	3¼″ × 22″	Door top shelf
J	1	3½″ × 22½″	Base
K	1	23¼″ × 80⅛″	Back
L	2	3″ × 11″	Drawer back
M	4	3¾″ × 12⅛″	Drawer side
N	2	10¾″ × 12⅛″	Drawer bottom
O	4	2″ × 3½″	Dividers
P	1	7″ × 20½″	Door shelf fascia
P1	1	3″ × 6¼″	Door shelf divider
Q	2	2″ × 20½″	Door shelf fascia
R	1	9″ × 22½″	Gun stock rack
S	1	4¼″ × 22½″	Barrel rack
T	2	2⅜″ × 2¾″ × 22½″	Gun shelf face
X	1	16¾″ × 22½″	Bottom shelf
	1		Hinge for barrel rack
	1		Lock for barrel rack
	1		Drawer lock
	1		Door bolt
	1	9″ × 22½″	Rubber or felt lining
	4		Pin hinges
		¼″ × 20½″ × 56″	Cork backing

Miscellaneous
4d and 6d finishing nails
Glue
Clips as required
Finishing materials

21
A Shelf Under the Window

House plants can get the benefit of summer sunshine and be attractive window ornaments if they're placed on window shelves.

The shelves are easy to make. The top of the window shelf is a piece of stepping 48″ long, with one rounded or "nosed" edge. Round the two ends by rasping and sanding to match the rounded edge.

Another piece of stepping is used for the braces. Make two squares, 11½″ × 11½″, and lay off a grid of 1″ squares, as shown in the drawing. Copy the curved pattern of the braces in pencil, and cut the braces out with a jigsaw or coping saw. With a rasp and sandpaper, smooth the curves and round the sharp edges.

The braces are attached to the shelf, 8″ from each end, using three No. 10 flathead wood screws, 2″ long, at each joint.

Cut a piece of 2 × 4 about 29⅞″ long to fit between the two braces. Fasten the 2 × 4 to the wall with the 4″ face against the wall. Then fasten the shelf board snugly against the wall and to the 2 × 4, using 2″ screws.

The window shelf should be painted to match or to contrast pleasingly with the finish of the building.

Materials List

1 piece, 1¼″ × 12″ × 4′ stepping
2 pieces, 1¼″ × 12″ × 12″
1 piece, 2″ × 4″ × 29⅞″
No. 10, 2″ flathead screws

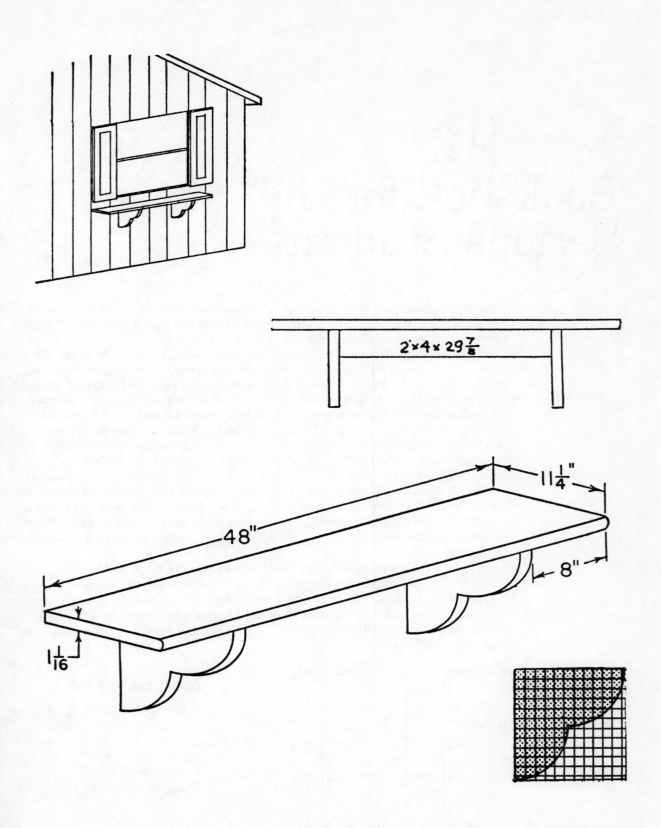

$2' \times 4 \times 29\frac{7}{8}$

$11\frac{1}{4}$"

48"

8"

$1\frac{1}{16}$

22
Bookshelf for the Serious Student

The simplest construction for a sturdy set of bookshelves calls for 1″ stock, which when planed is about ¾″ thick. A bookcase 36″ long and about 35″ high generally is ample for the use of most students.

First, make a plan drawing as shown in the accompanying sketches. This assists in drawing up a materials list, and helps when you discuss with your lumber dealer the kinds of woods best suited to the job. The bookshelf should blend with other furniture in the student's room; the selection of the wood, therefore, should take into consideration the finish desired.

For short shelf spans (up to 36″ long), finishing nails can support the normal book load without additional supports. For longer spans, it is desirable to provide shelf supports by placing small blocks beneath the shelf ends or by inserting vertical separators.

Few textbooks are taller than 9″ or 9½″, so place the shelves 10″ apart. If large books must be accommodated, the bottom shelf space may be made larger. This arrangement places the heavier books on the bottom where there is additional support; the "floor" of the bookcase is nailed on all four sides (see end view).

The heads of the long finishing nails are set into the wood and the holes are filled with plastic wood or other filler. Care should be taken to see that the filler material is not spread over the adjacent wood surface, especially if the natural grain of the wood is to be displayed in the finished case. Sanding removes any excess filler. In fact, the whole job should be sanded smoother before stain or varnish is applied.

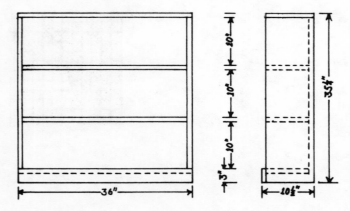

Materials List

2 pieces, 1″ × 10″ × 2′10½″
2 pieces, 1″ × 10″ × 3′
2 pieces, 1″ × 10″ × 2′10½″
1 piece, ½″ × 3″ × 3′
10d finishing nails
Paint, or stain and varnish

23
Bookcase: Colonial or Your Choice

The bookcase illustrated is distinctly colonial. The jigsawed valance at the top and the plinth (the low part of the base) establish that. If colonial is not your preference, all you have to do is change these two features to the style you want. For contemporary, for example, merely substitute straight line for the scrollwork described here.

To keep the colonial motif, use knotty pine random-width lumber. Ask your dealer for WP-4 with a V-groove. The molding at the top is standard crown molding, available at most retail lumberyards.

Start with the side pieces, cut and plane them to size, and sand both inside faces smooth. Mark the location of each shelf on the inside faces. Also mark and cut the notch on the upper front corner of each side to take the valance, which is $\frac{3}{4}'' \times 3\frac{5}{8}''$.

Cut the four shelves, plane to size, and sand. Fasten in place between the sides with glue and 8d finishing nails, setting the heads slightly.

The back is made up of five pieces of matched knotty pine. Cut stock to length. Then rip the two outer pieces and plane them to the required net width. Sand the face side of all panels carefully. Then nail the back to the two sides and to the rear edges of the shelves.

For the valance, make a paper pattern of the lower edge with the aid of the graph squares in the drawing, which shows the right-hand half. With a jig scroll saw, cut away the lower edge of this piece on the outline of the design. After it is cut out and sanded smoothly on face and edges, glue and nail it in the two side notches.

Cut and plane the top piece to size and sand smooth. Work a rabbet $\frac{5}{8}'' \times 1\frac{1}{4}''$ on the front edge and the two ends of this piece as shown in the section detail. On the back edge, rabbet $\frac{3}{8}'' \times \frac{3}{4}''$ to engage the back paneling.

Fasten the top in place with finishing nails driven into sides and valance, setting the heads afterward. Also nail the paneling in the rabbet on the back edge of the top member. The crown molding is cut into three pieces of the proper length, mitered at the two front corners. Locate the lower edge of this molding on a line $1\frac{3}{8}''$ below the underside of the top on sides and valance. Fasten it in place with $\frac{3}{4}''$ brads.

The plinth consists of three members with butting ends mitered. Also cut a chamfer ⅜" × ⅜" on the upper outside corner of each member. Make a pattern for the front jig-sawed member and trace it onto the plinth. Then cut it out and finish the edge in the same manner as the valance. Fasten the strip to the underside of the lower shelf, at the front edge, with three 1¼" screws. Nail the plinth members to the sides and along the strip.

When assembly is completed, sand the surfaces and apply sealer coat or stain. Either pine or maple stain may be used to simulate the mellow tone of colonial furniture. Fill the nail heads and then apply several coats of white shellac or clear flat varnish. When hard, the final coat should be rubbed down with pumice stone of No. 00 steel wool. If varnish is not used, apply several coats of paste wax, well rubbed, over the shellac. The resulting surface is quite durable.

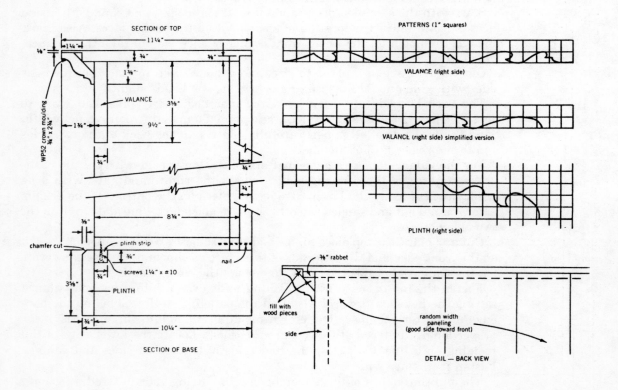

Materials List

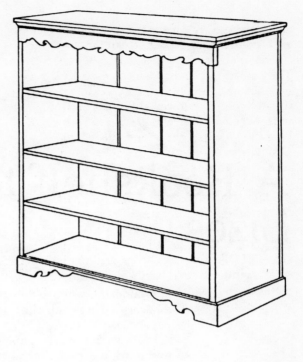

No.	Size	Use
2	1″ × 10″ × 48⅝″	Side pieces
4	1″ × 10″ × 42½″	Shelves
1	1″ × 12″ × 47½″	Top
1	1″ × 4″ × 44″	Valance
1	1″ × 4″ × 45½″	Front plinth
2	1″ × 4″ × 10¼″	Side plinths
1	¾″ × ¾″ × 42½″	Plinth strip

Knotty Pine Pattern WP-4

No.	Size	Use
1	1″ × 10″ × 45″	Groove one edge
1	1″ × 8″ × 45″	Tongue and groove
2	1″ × 10″ × 45″	Tongue and groove
1	1″ × 10″ × 45″	Tongue one edge

Miscellaneous

6′ Crown molding, WP-52, ¾″ × 2¾″
3 No. 10, 1¼″ flathead screws

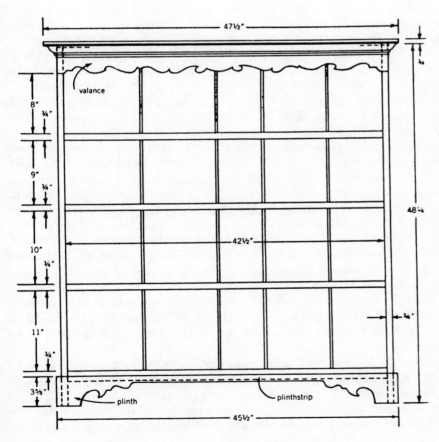

24
A Bookshelf for All Sizes

Wondering what to do with the variety of books you've collected? Here's the answer: a bookshelf that accommodates everything from big dictionaries to paperbacks.

Start with the side panels. Cut an 8′ × 12″ board exactly in half. Measure and mark a center line down the length of each panel. Strike a diagonal from the corner of one end to 1″ out from the center line on the other end. Do the same with a second diagonal, so that the top of the side panel is 2″ wide. Saw the diagonals with a crosscut to make a cleaner, less-jagged cut. Start the U-shaped cut at the bottom of each panel 2¼″ in from the edges. The crown of the U is 8½″ from the floor. Cut it out with a keyhole saw. File and sand the curved portion, top and bottom, until you are satisfied with the contour.

Measure and mark the distances separating each shelf, as indicated on the side view. Compute the shelf slant by allowing a 3¼″ height between heel and outer tip of the shelf, as shown on the bottom shelf of the side view.

Before attaching shelves to side panels, attach the bottom panel of each shelf to the corresponding back panel with 5 No. 5, 1½″ flathead wood screws and glue. Do this by placing the back panel in a vice and drilling ⅛″ holes through both panels at ends, center, and midpoint. Clean the surfaces, apply glue, and screw the panels together tightly. To keep the edge smooth, countersink holes before putting the screws in place. When the glue dries, the shelf is ready to attach to the side panels. Repeat this operation for the other three shelves.

Now clean the shelf edges. Position the shelves, one by one, on the side panel and nail them in place with 10d finishing nails. Repeat this step with the second side panel, as you go.

Next, carefully measure and cut 8 cleats from ¾ × ¾ stock. Drill ⅛″ holes to relieve No. 5, 1″ flathead wood screws, as shown in the side view. Countersink the holes, clean the surfaces, apply glue, and screw through the cleats into the shelf end side panel.

If you wish to add an extra touch for design's sake, plane the outer edges of each shelf perpendicular to the floor. Sand the entire unit lightly, taking care to clean all excess glue from surfaces. Set and fill nail holes.

As a permanent and decorative piece of furniture in the living room, the bookshelf deserves a good hardwood and fine oil finish. As a part of a colorful room for a child, there's every good reason to use a softwood and paint it a festive color.

Materials List

1 piece, 1″ × 12″ × 8′
2 pieces, 1″ × 4″ × 5′
2 pieces, 1″ × 5″ × 5′
2 pieces, 1″ × 6″ × 5′
2 pieces, 1″ × 8″ × 5′
1 piece, ¾″ × ¾″ × 3½′
3 doz. No. 5, 1″ flathead screws
2 doz. No. 5, 1½″ flathead wood screws
½ lb. 10d finishing nails
Glue

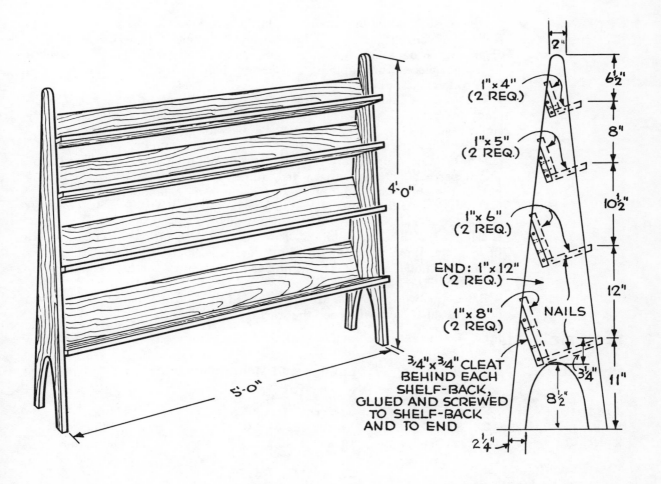

25
Dutch Buffet

Here's a handsome buffet you can build on a budget. And it's the place to store all of your elegant dining accessories. The upper cabinet has shelves for displaying china, knickknacks, heirlooms, and antiques. Each shelf is grooved to prevent pieces from slipping. The second shelf, with guard rail, is designed for a collection of plates.

The lower cabinet—31½″ high × 50″ wide × 20″ deep—provides space to display "treasures," a tea service, chafing dish, or wine font. Inside two roomy cupboards are slide trays that might be used for storing placemats and napkins, yet they are sturdy enough to accommodate the family silver chest. Beneath the trays are two large shelves for keeping table linens fresh and neat. The upper cabinet may be removed, allowing the unit to be used only as a buffet. Together, the height of the upper and lower cabinets is 71″.

Constructed with minimal framing lumber and ¾″ A-A, A-B, or B-B interior, or medium-density overlay (MDO) APA grade-trademarked plywood, the unit is trimmed with wood moldings. The recommended plywood grades require little or no preparation for finishing and are easily antiqued, stained, or painted to match a decor. The large back panel may even be wallpapered to accent the dining area.

Basic woodworking tools are all you need to build this buffet, but a power drill and saber saw will speed the work.

Materials List

Plywood

No.	Size
3 panels	¾″ × 4′ × 8′
1 panel	½″ × 4′ × 8′
2 pieces	⅜″ × 20¾″ × 25¾″

Miscellaneous

 4 pair offset hinges, decorative
 2 ceramic knobs
24 No. 10, 1¼″ flathead wood screws
 2 pair magnetic catches
6d finishing nails
Glue
Surfacing putty
Fine sandpaper
Paint or stain for finishing

Lumber and Molding

No.	Size	Use
3 pieces	½″ × ¾″ × 48″	Edging F
1 piece	2½″ × 6′	Molding for G1
1 piece	46½″	Molding for G2
2 pieces	¾″ × ¾″ × 46½″	Screw strips 0
2 pieces	¾″ × ¾″ × 15″	Screw strips P
4 pieces	23⅝″ (24″ cut to fit, mitered)	Molding for D5
4 pieces	18⅝″ (19″, same)	Molding for D6
4 pieces	19″ (20″, same)	Molding for D7
4 pieces	14″ (15″, same)	Molding for D8
8 pieces	¼″ × ½″ × 15¾″	Gliders T3
1 piece	$1^1/_{16}$″ × 2¼″ × 16½″	Center guides T6
2 pieces	$1^1/_{16}$″ × $^{29}/_{16}$″ × 16½″	Side guides T7

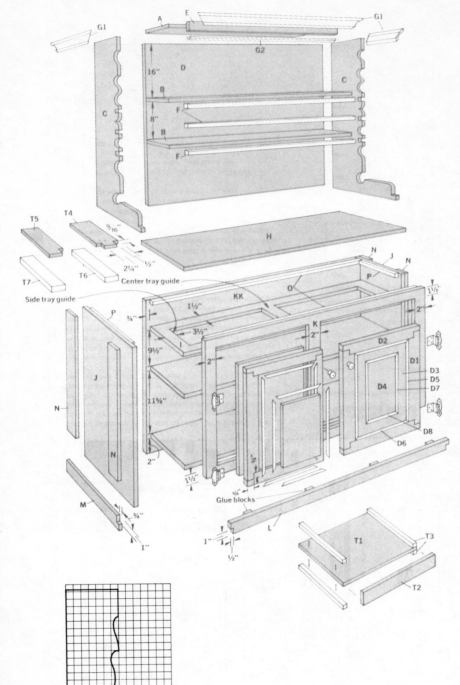

UPPER CABINET

A — Top 1 pc. ¾" x 5½" x 46½"

B — Shelves 2 pcs. ¾" x 5¾" x 46½"

C — Ends 2 pcs. ¾" x 13½" x 38¼"

D — Back 1 pc. ¾" x 38¼" x 46½"

E — Facing 1 pc. ¾" x 3" x 46½"

F — Edgings 3 pcs. ½" x ¾" x 48"

G1 — Crown Molding 1 pc. 2½" Cove 6' (Miter to fit)

G2 — Molding 1 pc. 46½"

LOWER CABINET

H — Top 1 pc. ¾" x 19½" x 50"

I — Shelves 3 pcs. ¾" x 16½" x 46½"

J — Ends 2 pcs. ¾" x 16½" x 31"

K — Front 1 pc. ¾" x 29" x 48"

DOOR OPENING — 21" wide x 26" height

KK — Back 1 pc. ¾" x 31" x 48"

L — Base 1 pc. ¾" x 2" x 49"

M — Base 2 pcs. ½" x 2" x 18"

N — End trim 4 pcs. ½" x 2" x 29"

O — Screw strips 2 pcs. ¾" x ¾" x 46½"

P — Screw strips 2 pcs. ¾" x ¾" x 15"

DOORS

D1 — Stiles 4 pcs. ¾" x 1½" x 25⅛"

D2 — Rails 4 pcs. ¾" x 1½" x 21⅝"

D3 — Panel 2 pcs. ⅜" x 20¾" x 25¾"

D4 — Panel 2 pcs. ½" x 13" x 18"

D5 — Moldings 4 pcs. 23⅝"   24"

D6 — Moldings 4 pcs. 18⅝"   19"

D7 — Moldings 4 pcs. 19"   20"

D8 — Moldings 4 pcs. 14"   15"

SILVER TRAYS

T1 — Bottoms 2 pcs. ½" x 15¾" x 19½"

T2 — Fronts 2 pcs. ½" x 2½" x 19½"

T3 — Glider 8 pcs. ¼" x ½" x 15¾"

T4 — Center Guide 1 pc. ½" x 3¼" x 16½"

T5 — Side Guide 2 pcs. ½" x 3 1/16" x 16½"

T6 — Center guide 1 pc. 1 1/16" x 2¼" x 16½"

T7 — Side guide 2 pcs. 1 1/16" x 2 9/16" x 16½"

detail

Layout Grid (C)
Each square represents 1"

upper

lower

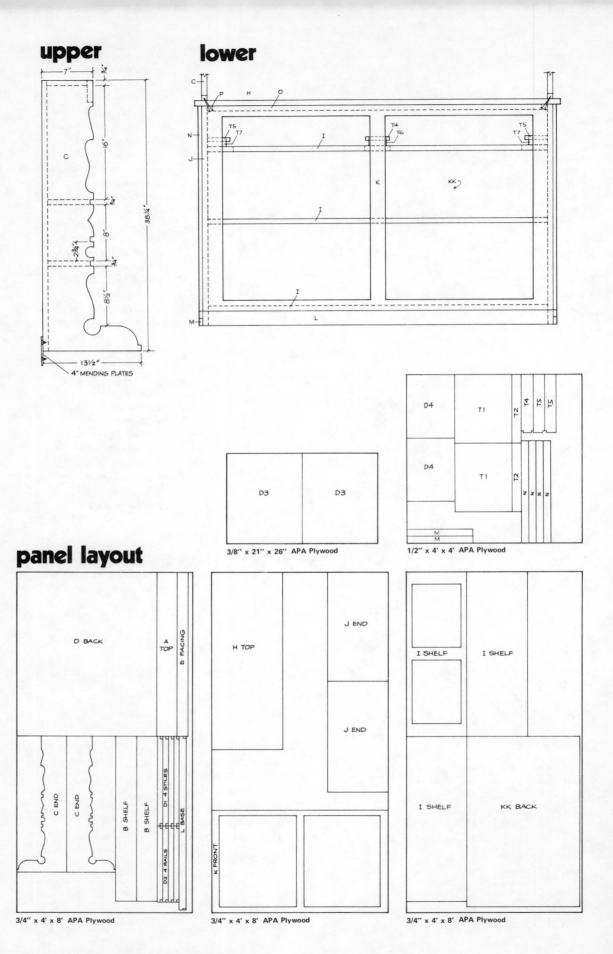

3/8" x 21" x 26" APA Plywood

1/2" x 4' x 4' APA Plywood

panel layout

3/4" x 4' x 8' APA Plywood

3/4" x 4' x 8' APA Plywood

3/4" x 4' x 8' APA Plywood

26
Sewing and Hobby Center

The trouble with most hobbies is that they don't stay small. First the hobby paraphernalia is on a desk, then in a corner of a room, and then scattered all over the house. This new sewing and hobby center can put an end to all this disorganization.

Closed, the 78″ high center is a sleek piece of contemporary furniture just 40″ wide and 13″ deep. Opened, it's 80″ wide and has a wealth of storage space. Both doors are 9½″ deep and are organized into several sizes of shelved compartments.

The center of the unit has a hinged, flip-down counter for a sewing work surface. The sewing machine, mounted in a lipped box, is stored on the shelf and drops into a well in the shelf for use. The pegboard behind the counter is a great place to hang small sewing or hobby tools. The shelves above are perfect for larger supplies, a work lamp, and books.

It takes 7 sheets of APA grade-trademarked plywood, standard woodworking tools, and basic carpentry skills to put you on the way to a small, compact hobby center.

Materials List

Plywood

No.	Size
6 panels	½″ × 4′ × 8′
1 panel	¾″ × 4′ × 8′

Other Materials

5 Piano hinges
2 pieces, 77″ long for front doors
2 pieces, 14″ long for shelf supports
1 piece, 56″ long for ironing-board door
1 piece, 37″ long for work shelf

1 piece, ¼″ × 32″ × 17½″ pegboard
4 magnetic catches and plates
⅛″ × 1″ aluminum barnstock to measure of machine base perimeter (optional)
No. 6 screws for attaching bar stock to box (optional)
6d finishing nails
White glue or urea-resin glue
Wood dough or surfacing putty
Fine sandpaper
Paint, stain, or antiquing for finish

panel layout

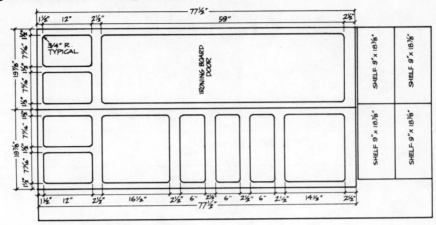

1/2" x 4' x 8' APA plywood

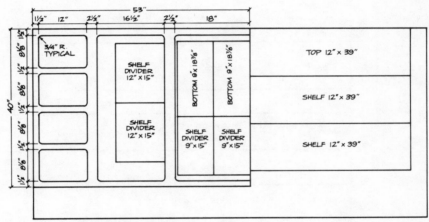

1/2" x 4' x 8' APA plywood

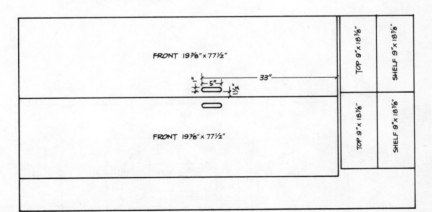

1/2" x 4' x 8' APA plywood

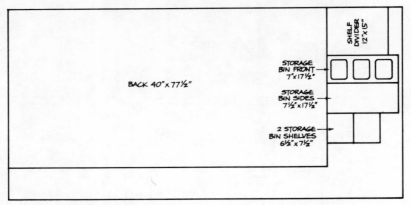

1/2'' x 4' x 8' APA plywood

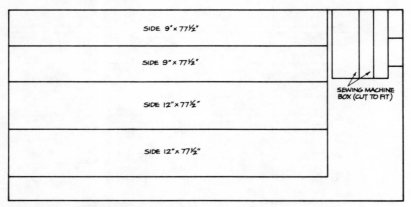

1/2'' x 4' x 8' APA plywood

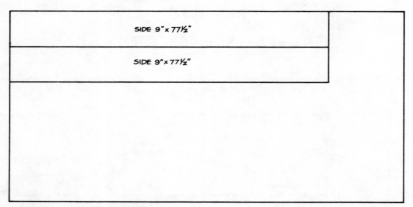

1/2'' x 4' x 8' APA plywood

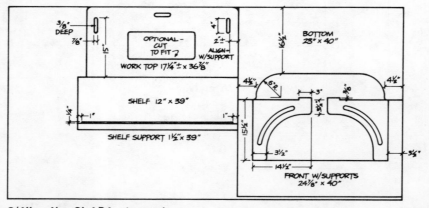

3/4'' x 4' x 8' APA plywood

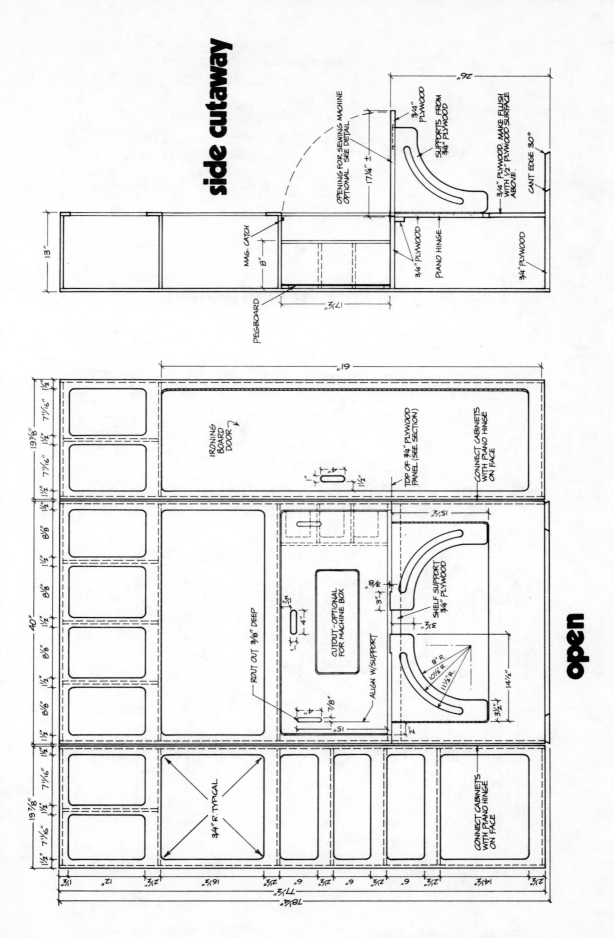

side cutaway

open

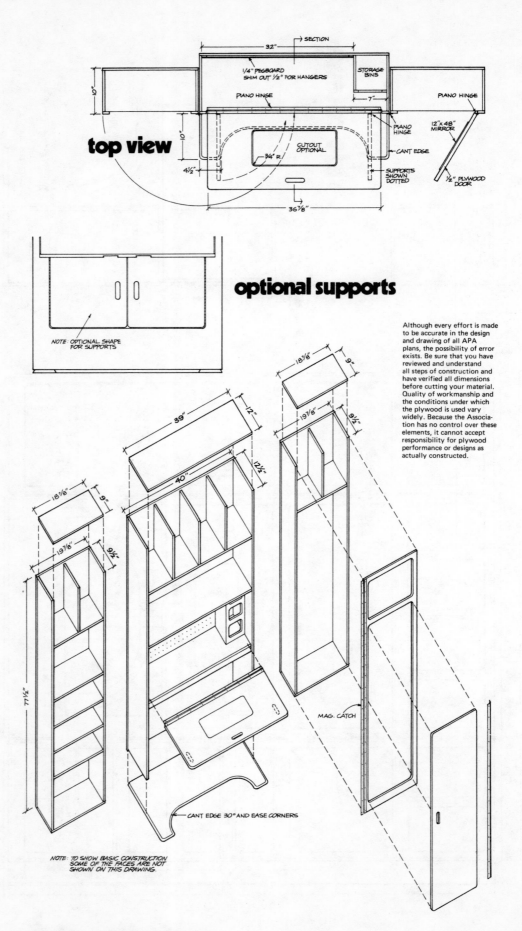

top view

SECTION

32"

1/4" PEGBOARD
SHIM OUT 1/2" FOR HANGERS

STORAGE BINS

10"

PIANO HINGE

7"

PIANO HINGE

10"

CUTOUT OPTIONAL

12" x 48" MIRROR

3/4" R

PIANO HINGE

4 1/2"

CANT EDGE

SUPPORTS SHOWN DOTTED

1/2" PLYWOOD DOOR

36 1/8"

optional supports

NOTE: OPTIONAL SHAPE FOR SUPPORTS

Although every effort is made to be accurate in the design and drawing of all APA plans, the possibility of error exists. Be sure that you have reviewed and understand all steps of construction and have verified all dimensions before cutting your material. Quality of workmanship and the conditions under which the plywood is used vary widely. Because the Association has no control over these elements, it cannot accept responsibility for plywood performance or designs as actually constructed.

18 1/8"

9"

12"

19 7/8"

9 1/2"

39"

12 1/2"

40"

18 1/8"

9"

19 7/8"

9 1/2"

77 1/2"

MAG. CATCH

CANT EDGE 30° AND EASE CORNERS

NOTE: TO SHOW BASIC CONSTRUCTION SOME OF THE FACES ARE NOT SHOWN ON THIS DRAWING.

back panel

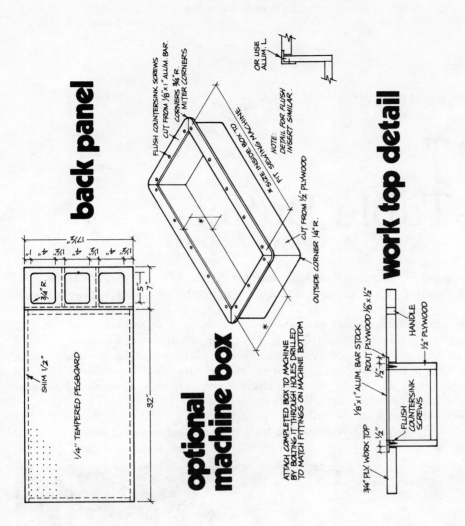

back panel

1/4" TEMPERED PEGBOARD

SHIM 1/2"

3/4" R.

17 3/4"

1" 4" 3 1/4" 3 1/4" 4" 1 3/4"

5"
7"
32"

optional machine box

FLUSH COUNTERSINK SCREWS

CUT FROM 1/8" x 1" ALUM. BAR.

CORNERS 3/4" R.

MITER CORNERS

FIT SEWING MACHINE

* SIZE INSIDE BOX

CUT FROM 1/2" PLYWOOD

OUTSIDE CORNER 1/4" R.

OR USE ALUM. L

NOTE:
DETAIL FOR FLUSH
INSERT SIMILAR.

ATTACH COMPLETED BOX TO MACHINE
BY BOLTING IT THROUGH HOLES DRILLED
TO MATCH FITTINGS ON MACHINE BOTTOM

work top detail

1/8" x 1" ALUM. BAR STOCK

ROUT PLYWOOD 1/8" x 1/2"

1/2"

HANDLE

1/2" PLYWOOD

FLUSH
COUNTERSINK
SCREWS

1/2"

3/4" PLY WORK TOP

front w/doors closed

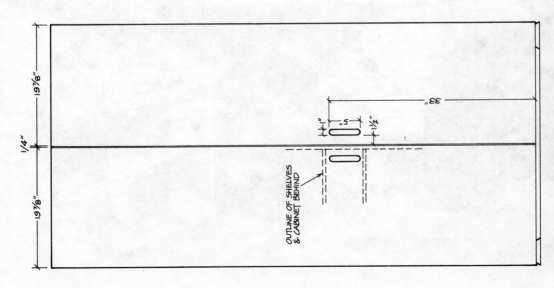

19 7/8"

1/4"

19 7/8"

OUTLINE OF SHELVES
& CABINET BEHIND

1"
5"
1/2"

33"

27
Dining-Table Buffet

Designed for convenience, this dining-table buffet is a serving table, bar, storage center—everything you need for enjoyable entertaining in a single package you can build yourself.

The dining-table buffet consists of three units: a drop-leaf table and two rolling carts. When the drop leaf is down, the whole thing takes up space of only 2′ × 6′ × 30¼″. With the leaf up, there's a 39″ wide tabletop and serving space. One under-the-counter storage cart has three 15″ × 21¼″ drawers and a spacious shelf. The other cart has three roomy shelves. Both can double as serving units to supplement the main table.

The entire dining-table buffet can be built by an experienced do-it-yourselfer for under $130. Basic woodworking tools plus a saber saw and plywood are all you need.

Materials List

Plywood

No.	Size
1 panel	⅜″ × 4′ × 8′
1 piece	⅜″ × 2′ × 4′ (Ask your dealer about availability of cut-to-size or partial panels.)
2 panels	⅝″ × 4′ × 8′

Lumber

Size	Quantity	Use
2″ × 2″	32′	Tabletop framing
1″ × 1″	77′	Tabletop frames, cleats, leg, leaf support framing
1″ × 2″	30′	Leg and leaf support framing
1″ × 3″	8′	Interior framing
1″ × 4″ (ripped to 3″)	7′	Interior framing
2″ × 4″ (ripped to 2½″)	5′	Interior framing

Hardware

No.		Use
1 piece	21″ × 69″ plastic laminate	Top
2 pieces	9″ × 69″ plastic laminate	Leaf top and bottom
2	28″ piano hinges	Leaf supports
4	3″ butt hinges	Leaf top
6 pairs	22″ drawer slides	
8	2″ casters	
6	2½″ carriage bolts	

Miscellaneous
4d finishing nails
8d finishing nails
No. 8, 2½″ flathead wood screws (approx. 9)
No. 8, 1″ flathead wood screws (approx. 9)
White glue
Wood dough or filler
Fine sandpaper
Top-quality paint or antiquing
    materials for finishing

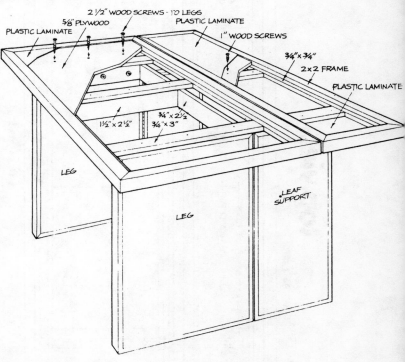

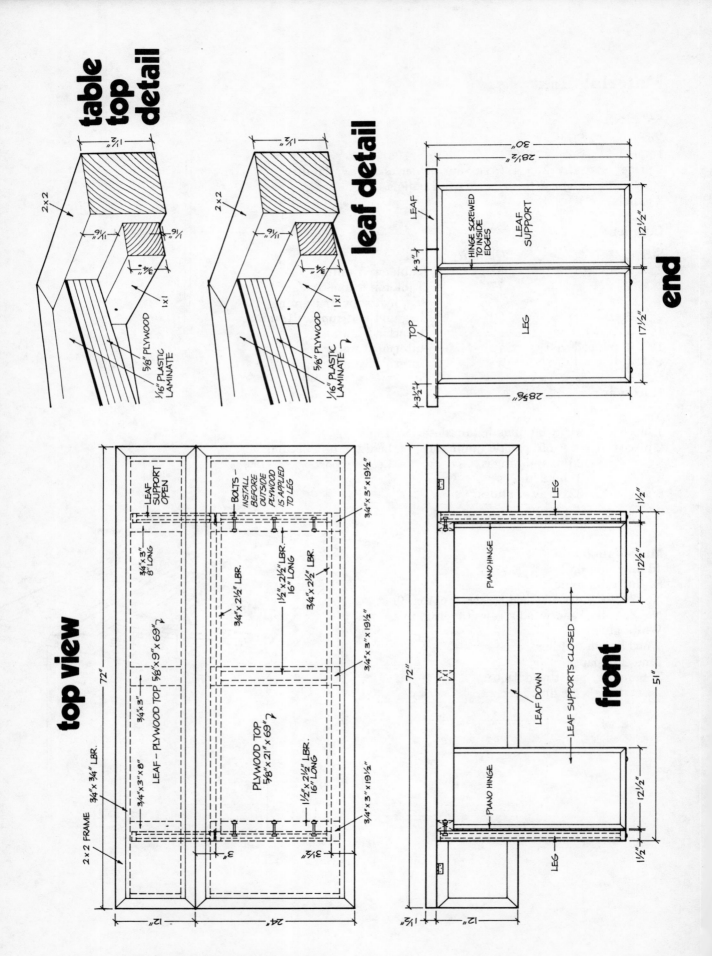

table top detail

2x2

1½"

1 1/16"   1 1/16"

⅝" PLYWOOD

1/16" PLASTIC LAMINATE

1x1

¾"

2x2

1½"

1 1/16"

⅝" PLYWOOD

1/16" PLASTIC LAMINATE

1x1

¾"

leaf detail

end

30"

28½"

LEAF

HINGE SCREWED TO INSIDE EDGES

LEAF SUPPORT

LEG

3"

TOP

3½"

12½"

17½"

28⅜"

top view

72"

LEAF SUPPORT OPEN

BOLTS — INSTALL BEFORE OUTSIDE PLYWOOD IS APPLIED TO LEG

¾" x 3" 8" LONG

LEAF — PLYWOOD TOP ⅝" x 9" x 69"

¾" x 3"

¾" x 2½" LBR.

1½" x 2½" LBR. 16" LONG

¾" x 2½" LBR.

¾" x 3" x 19½"

¾" x 3" x 19½"

PLYWOOD TOP ⅝" x 21" x 69"

1½" x 2½" LBR. 16" LONG

¾" x 3" x 19½"

2x2 FRAME

¾" x ¾" LBR.

¾" x 3" x 8"

3"

3½"

12"

24"

front

72"

51"

LEG

PIANO HINGE

LEAF DOWN

LEAF SUPPORTS CLOSED

PIANO HINGE

LEG

1½"

12½"

12½"

1½"

1½"

12"

shelf cart

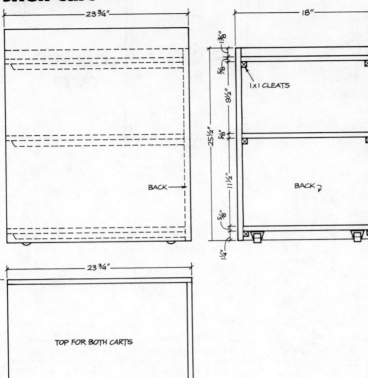

23¾"

1⅜"
⅝"
9½"
25½"
⅝"
11½"
⅝"
1¼"
18"
28"

1 x 1 CLEATS

BACK →

BACK ⌐

23¾"

18"

TOP FOR BOTH CARTS

drawer cart

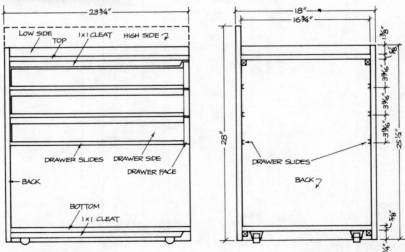

23¾"

LOW SIDE   TOP   1 x 1 CLEAT   HIGH SIDE ⌐

DRAWER SLIDES   DRAWER SIDE

DRAWER FACE

← BACK

BOTTOM
1 x 1 CLEAT

18"
16¾"
1⅜"
⅝"
3¾₆"
3¾₆"
3¾₆"
28"
25½"
⅝"
1¼"

DRAWER SLIDES

BACK ⌐

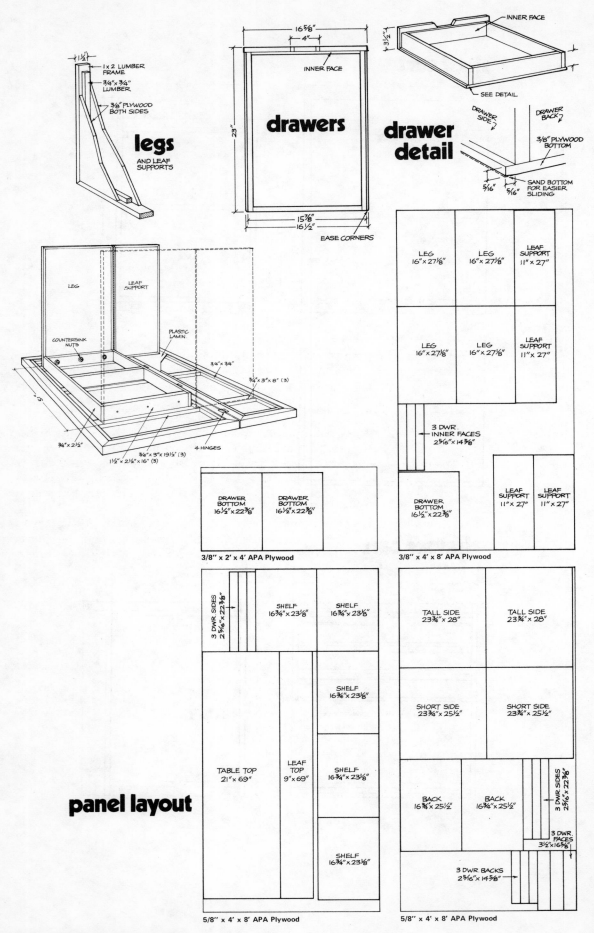

legs

AND LEAF SUPPORTS

1 x 2 LUMBER FRAME

3/4" x 3/4" LUMBER

3/8" PLYWOOD BOTH SIDES

drawers

16 5/8"

4"

INNER FACE

23"

15 7/8"

16 1/2"

EASE CORNERS

drawer detail

INNER FACE

3 1/2"

SEE DETAIL

DRAWER SIDE

DRAWER BACK

3/8" PLYWOOD BOTTOM

5/16"   5/16"

SAND BOTTOM FOR EASIER SLIDING

LEG

LEAF SUPPORT

COUNTERSINK NUTS

PLASTIC LAMIN.

3/4" x 3/4"

3/4" x 3" x 8" (3)

15"

3/4" x 2 1/2"

3/4" x 3" x 19 1/2" (3)

1 1/2" x 2 1/2" x 16" (3)

4 HINGES

| LEG 16" x 27 1/8" | LEG 16" x 27 1/8" | LEAF SUPPORT 11" x 27" |
| LEG 16" x 27 1/8" | LEG 16" x 27 1/8" | LEAF SUPPORT 11" x 27" |

3 DWR. INNER FACES 2 5/16" x 14 5/8"

DRAWER BOTTOM 16 1/2" x 22 3/8"

LEAF SUPPORT 11" x 27"

LEAF SUPPORT 11" x 27"

3/8" x 4' x 8' APA Plywood

| DRAWER BOTTOM 16 1/2" x 22 3/8" | DRAWER BOTTOM 16 1/2" x 22 3/8" |

3/8" x 2' x 4' APA Plywood

panel layout

3 DWR SIDES 2 5/16" x 22 3/8"

| SHELF 16 3/4" x 23 1/8" | SHELF 16 3/4" x 23 1/8" |

SHELF 16 3/4" x 23 1/8"

| TABLE TOP 21" x 69" | LEAF TOP 9" x 69" |

SHELF 16 3/4" x 23 1/8"

SHELF 16 3/4" x 23 1/8"

5/8" x 4' x 8' APA Plywood

TALL SIDE 23 3/4" x 28"	TALL SIDE 23 3/4" x 28"
SHORT SIDE 23 3/4" x 25 1/2"	SHORT SIDE 23 3/4" x 25 1/2"
BACK 16 3/4" x 25 1/2"	BACK 16 3/4" x 25 1/2"

3 DWR SIDES 2 5/16" x 22 3/8"

3 DWR. FACES 3 1/2" x 16 5/8"

3 DWR. BACKS 2 5/16" x 14 5/8"

5/8" x 4' x 8' APA Plywood

28
Kitchen Storage Cart

If you have more small appliances and kitchen equipment than you have counterspace or cupboards, take heart. Here's a handy movable storage cart for frequently used, bulky items like slow-cookers, blenders, toasters, waffle irons, or popcorn poppers. And there's a vertical compartment, sized for storing big cutting boards.

However, this is more than just a repository for kitchen tools. Finished on top with plastic laminate, the cart doubles as a food preparation center comprising 864 square inches of work space. It's also a mobile serving cart at mealtimes or a portable bar for parties. Mounted on heavy-duty globe casters, the cart is easily rolled from the kitchen to the dining room, family room, or patio.

A reasonably skilled do-it-yourselfer can construct the cart. All it takes is two panels of APA grade-trademarked plywood, four casters, a pull-bar, plastic laminate, and some nails and screws. Only basic woodworking tools are required, but a saber saw will speed the work.

Materials List

2 panels, ¾″ × 4′ × 8′ plywood
1 set, 1½″ heavy-duty globe casters
1 piece, 23⅞″ × 36″ plastic laminate for top
2 pieces, 3″ × 36″ plastic laminate for side
2 pieces, 3″ × 23⅞″ plastic laminate for ends
10′ 1″ × 1″ lumber for shelf support cleats
1 pull bar, 1″ in diameter × 18″ long
4d finishing nails
6d finishing nails
White or urea-resin glue
Wood dough or filler
Fine sandpaper
Paint, stain, or antiquing for finishing

exploded view

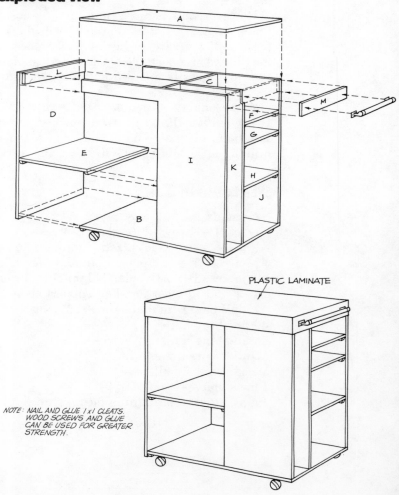

PLASTIC LAMINATE

NOTE: NAIL AND GLUE 1x1 CLEATS.
WOOD SCREWS AND GLUE
CAN BE USED FOR GREATER
STRENGTH.

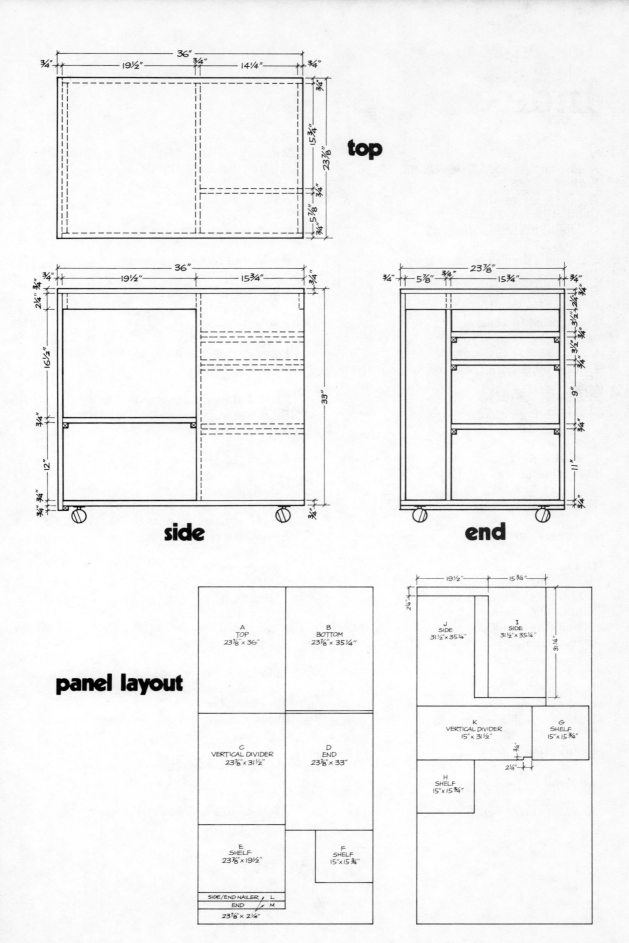

top

side

end

panel layout

A
TOP
23⅞″ × 36″

B
BOTTOM
23⅞″ × 35¼″

C
VERTICAL DIVIDER
23⅞″ × 31½″

D
END
23⅞″ × 33″

E
SHELF
23⅞″ × 19½″

F
SHELF
15″ × 15¾″

SIDE/END NAILER   L
END   M
23⅞″ × 2¼″

J
SIDE
31½″ × 35¼″

I
SIDE
31½″ × 35¼″

K
VERTICAL DIVIDER
15″ × 31½″

G
SHELF
15″ × 15¾″

H
SHELF
15″ × 15¾″

Index